TOP INSTANT POT RECIPES COOKBOOK

Fresh & Foolproof Pressure Cooker Recipes for Smart People

BY

Clara Michael

ISBN: 978-1-952504-58-7

COPYRIGHT © 2020 by Clara Michael

All rights reserved. This book is copyright protected and it's for personal use only. Without the prior written permission of the publisher, no part of this publication should be reproduced, distributed, or transmitted in any form or by any means, including photocopying, recording, or other electronic or mechanical methods.

This publication is sold with the idea that the publisher is not required to render accounting, officially permitted, or otherwise, qualified services. If advise is required, it is necessary to seek the services of a legal or professional, a practiced individual in the profession. This document is geared towards providing substantial and reliable information in regards to the topics covered.

DISCLAIMER

The information written in this book is for educational and entertainment purposes only. Strenuous efforts have been made to provide accurate, up to date and reliable complete information. The information in this book is true and complete to the best of our knowledge. All recommendations are made without guarantee on the part of the author and publisher.

Neither the publisher nor the author takes any responsibility for any possible consequences of reading or enjoying the recipes in this book. The author and publisher disclaim any liability in connection with the use of information contained in this book. Under no circumstance will any legal responsibility or blame be apportioned against the author or publisher for any reparation, damages, or monetary loss due to the information herein, either directly or indirectly.

Table of Contents

INTRODUCTION 8
   Meaning of Instant Pot 8
Benefits of Cooking with an Instant Pot 9
Function Keys of Your Instant Pot 11
Steps to Effectively Clean Your Instant Pot 14
INSTANT POT BREAKFAST RECIPES 16
   Breakfast Porridge 16
   Instant Pot Congee 18
   Apple Cinnamon Steel Cut Oats 19
   Breakfast Burritos 20
   Strawberry Trail Mix Oatmeal 21
   Cinnamon Roll French Toast Casserole 22
   Quinoa Breakfast Bowls 24
   Tempeh Breakfast Bowl 25
   Blueberry Oatmeal 27
   Buckwheat Porridge 28
   Mexican Breakfast Casserole 29
   Cinnamon Crunch Oatmeal 31
   Breakfast Potatoes 32
   Lemon Blueberry Breakfast Cake 34
   Cinnamon Banana Oatmeal 36
INSTANT POT SOUP & STEW RECIPES 37
   French Onion Soup 37
   Spicy Ethiopian Stew 38
   Cheeseburger Soup 39
   Andouille Sausage Stew 40
   Creamed Fennel and Cauliflower Soup 41

    Pork and Hominy Stew 42

    Swiss Chard Stem Soup 43

    Green Chile Stew 44

    Butternut Cauliflower Soup 46

    Italian Beef Stew 47

    Cheddar Broccoli Potato Soup 48

    Spicy Beef Stew 49

    Stuffed Pepper Soup 50

INSTANT POT POULTRY RECIPES 52

    Chicken Noodle Soup 52

    Chicken Taco Soup 53

    Chicken Cacciatore 54

    Chicken Cordon Bleu 56

    BBQ Chicken with Potatoes 57

    Chicken Chile Verde 58

    Pineapple Chicken Breasts 59

    Orange Chicken 60

    Chicken Marsala 62

    Honey Garlic Chicken 64

    General Tso's Chicken 65

    Chicken Adobo 67

    Teriyaki Chicken and Rice 68

    Salsa Lime Chicken 69

    Honey Mustard Curry Chicken 70

INSTANT POT BEEF & PORK RECIPES 71

    Pulled Pork Tacos 71

    Beer-Braised Pulled Ham 72

    Beef Masala Curry 73

Japanese Pork Tender Rib Stew 74
Cuban Shredded Beef Stew 76
Pork and Pineapple Stew 78
Hoisin Meatballs 80
Beef Curry 81
Pork Vindaloo 82
Beef Chili 84
Easy Pork Posole 85
Mesquite Ribs 86
Pork Chops with Gravy 87

INSTANT POT FISH & SEAFOOD RECIPES 89
Steamed Alaskan Crab Legs 89
Lemon Pepper Salmon 90
Bang Bang Shrimp Pasta 91
Sweet and Spicy Pineapple Shrimp 92
Shrimp Paella 93
Fish Tacos 94
Drunken Clams 95
Seafood Gumbo 96
Chipotle Shrimp Soup 98
Shrimp Scampi Paella 100

INSTANT POT EGG RECIPES 101
Breakfast Egg Casserole 101
Eggs in Marinara Sauce 103
Perfect Poached Egg 104
Crustless Quiche 105
Ham and Egg Casserole 106
Cheesy Egg Bake 107

    Mexican Egg Casserole 108

    Hard Boiled Eggs 109

    Mini Frittatas 110

    Eggs en Cocotte 111

INSTANT POT BEAN & GRAIN RECIPES 112

    Lora's Red Beans & Rice 112

    Spanish Rice with Beef Sirloin or Flank Steak 113

    Mexican Beef Rice 114

    Black Bean & Rice Burritos 115

    Pinto Beans 116

    Refried Beans 117

    Mexican Rice with Corn and Bell Peppers 118

    Hamburger and Rice 119

INSTANT POT VEGAN & VEGETARIAN RECIPES 120

    Potato Corn Chowder 120

    Vegan BBQ Meatballs 122

    Pasta Puttanesca 123

    Garlic Hummus 124

    Lentil Soup 125

    Pulled BBQ Jackfruit 126

    Black Bean Soup 127

    Vegetable Bolognese 128

    Cilantro Lime Quinoa 130

    Mashed Potatoes with Fried Onions and Bacon 131

INSTANT POT APPETIZER RECIPES 132

    Cocktail Wieners 132

    Honey BBQ Wings 133

    Cilantro Lime Drumsticks 134

Bacon Cheeseburger Dip 135

Jalapeno Hot Popper & Chicken Dip 136

Artichoke and Spinach Dip 137

BBQ Pulled Pork Sliders 138

Chili Con Queso 139

Pizza Pull Apart Bread 140

Sweet and Spicy Meatballs 141

INSTANT POT DESSERT RECIPES 142

Molten Mocha Cake 142

Cherry & Spice Rice Pudding 143

Chocolate Pots de Crème 144

Black and Blue Cobbler 145

Arroz Con Leche 147

Pumpkin Pie Pudding 148

Key Lime Pie 149

INTRODUCTION

Meaning of Instant Pot

The Instant Pot is an electronic cooking device or machine programmed to perform the function of 7 gadgets. Unlike electric pressure cooker, steamer, slow cooker, yoghurt maker, rice cooker, warming pot or sauté pan, Instant Pot is a cooker programmed with multi-functions which can perform the same task like the afore mentioned machines. The Instant Pot is a seven-in-one multi cooker combined that can work as an electric pressure cooker, steamer, slow cooker, yoghurt maker, rice cooker, and sauté pan. It can cook meals instantly and faster but it has an option for a start time that can be programmed to delay.

Some people that likes convenient cooking and the option of "set it and forget it" in a slow cooker would have a great passion for Instant Pot and also including those who desires to have a pressure cooker, steamer, yoghurt maker and slow cooker simultaneously but has little or no space to occupy the four cookers, Instant Pot performs the same functions like the other four machines. The Instant Pot comes with instruction manual and short booklet of recipes which contain functions of Instant Pot and manufacturer's recommended quantities of food ingredients together with preparation and cooking times to help the newbies.

The Instant Pot will save you a whole lot of time if you want to cook food like stew, lentils or grains. The special thing about Instant Pot is that it has a lot of functional uses for a single appliance and you can set it and walk away doing other things while the machine does its magic. With its multi-functional ability, it may seem difficult to operate your Instant Pot but it's very easy to operate when you follow the instruction manual.

Benefits of Cooking with an Instant Pot

1. It Can Cook Beans Super-Fast.

This reason alone got my attention to this fabulous Instant Pot device. While it takes some people about 12-15 minutes to cook soaked beans and 37-40 minutes to cook dry beans. I was not fully convinced when the Instant Pot cook beans very fast until I heard it over and over again from different people and their good comments made about their Instant Pot. That was when I started having great passion for Instant Pot and it earned a space in my kitchen.

2. To Make Perfect Brown Rice.

It's not easy to cook brown rice but it was easy for me. I have been thinking brown rice was easy to cook but was doubtful the first time I cooked brown rice with little water and I thought I would made crunchy rice. However, the rice was not crunchy as I thought and it was perfect rice I have ever cooked. You can use your Instant Pot to make recipes like Mexican Casserole, Cheesy Broccoli and Rice Casserole perfectly in a fraction of the time.

3. Steam/Cook Veggies in Minutes.

The Instant Pot cooks veggies in minutes. When cooking veggies, do not walk away to avoid burning or overcooking your veggies. It's important to stick to the step by step recipes instructions when cooking veggies. I've burned more than my fair share of veggies by forgetting about them. You have to make use of quick pressure release to release the steam once they are finished cooking.

4. Built in Timer.

What amazes me the most about the Instant Pot machine is the fact that you can cook a meal, walk away and come back later to meet fully cooked meals. The Instant Pot will not start cooking by itself until you want it to cook by using the timer. You can program your dinner to start at 4:30pm and keep it warm until you get home.

5. Easy Clean Up.

Washing of my dishes is one of the things I have little time to do. I do avoid cooking dishes that will require thorough washing of dishes. When it comes to Instant Pot, it is very easy to clean up after use.

6. Pressure Cooking Retains More Nutrients.

Researchers have it that food cooked for a short time with less water retains more nutrients. Instant Pot retains more nutrients because of its short duration used for cooking. Due to the high pressure, beans and grains become more digestible.

7. They are Safe.

There are some reports on injuries or dangers of pressure cookers blowing up while cooking. Some people became scared of using pressure cooker because of some domestic violence caused by the pressure cooker. However, Instant Pot is very safe to use. It has 10 in-built safety features which include high temperature warning, a lid which is to be locked while cooking, automatic pressure control and many others.

8. Slow Cooker.

The Instant Pot is a little taller but has the same size with slow cookers. The Instant Pot also perform the function of a slow cooker by just pressing a button. Some people may decide to use their Instant Pot as a slow cooker on regular bases. By doing this, you must make sure you buy the optional lid so you can be able to use the Instant Pot as a slow cooker on regular basis.

9. Sauté feature.

The Instant Pot has a sauté feature. It means the Instant Pot can also perform the function of a sauté pan. So you can toss onions and garlic in, select sauté button, prepare the rest of your ingredients and then add them to the pot and set the time you want Instant Pot to cook whatever you wants to cook.

Function Keys of Your Instant Pot

1. **Manual / Pressure Buttons:**

    This function will be frequently used which enables you to select the cooking time manually and pressure cook what you wants to cook. The Instant Pot pressure, time and temperature can be adjusted by pressing the "+/-" features. It is imperative to follow the recipe instructions to know if you are to pressure cook the food using Low or High Pressure. The "Manual" and "Pressure" button stands for pressure cooking unlike functions like "Sauté", "Yogurt" or "Slow cooker" which does not require pressure cooking. The Instant Pot's default setting is High Pressure when you press the "Manual" button.

2. **Sauté Button:**

    This feature is the second most frequently used button on the Instant Pot. You can select the sauté button to cook up anything as you would in a skillet or pan without 1 cup of liquid. All you need to do is just to set the "Sauté" button, add some cooking oil like butter, avocado, coconut or animal fat like beef tallow or lard to the inner pot and add food you want to cook like a skillet or pan. The sauté button can be used to cook ingredients like onion, garlic and meat. Most times, I start with the "Sauté" function and then use the "Manual" / "Pressure" button to pressure cook my meal.

3. **Slow Cook Button:**

    This button helps you to use Instant Pot like a slower cooker. This function allows the Instant Pot to perform the function of a slow cooker. Just add food as you normally do to a slow cooker, secure the lid and then select the "Slow Cook" button and use "+/-" buttons to adjust the cook time.

4. **Bean / Chili:**

    This button allows the Instant Pot to cook beans faster than any other cooker. This is why beans is the food I like cooking most in my Instant Pot. The "Bean / Chili" button, uses the default High Pressure for 30 minutes though it can be adjusted for "More" to High Pressure for 35 minutes or "Less" for High Pressure for 20 minutes. Black beans take about 10-15 minutes, while kidney beans take 20-25. The Instant Pot Manual has different cooking times for various beans and legumes.

5. **Meat / Stew:**

    The Instant Pot can easily make your favorite stew or meat dish. It can make it by adjusting the settings depending on the desired texture. For instance, a homemade stew with about 1-2 lb. of meat, you can set it to "Meat / Stew" button using high pressure for 35 minutes. The "More" setting is great for fall-off-the-bone cooking. It will set to a default High Pressure for 35 minutes. The Instant Pot can be adjusted for "More" to High Pressure for 45 minutes or "Less" for High Pressure for 20 minutes.

6. **Multigrain:**

   This function can be used for cooking wild rice or brown rice which usually takes longer time than cooking white rice. Cook brown rice to a 1:1.25 ratio rice to water and wild rice to a 1:3 ratio rice to water for 25-30 minutes. The default (Normal) setting is 40 minutes of cooking time but can be adjusted as required for the "Less" setting to 20 minutes of cooking time, or "More" at 45 minutes of warm water soaking and 60 minutes of cooking.

7. **Porridge:**

   Rice porridge (congee) and other grains can be cooked using the porridge button.

The default cooking time on High Pressure for rice porridge is 20 minutes but can be adjusted for "More" to High Pressure for 30 minutes or "Less" for High Pressure for 15 minutes. When the cooking cycle has completed, it is not advisable to use Quick Pressure Release because it has high starch content and may splatter the porridge through the steam release vent. It's imperative to use the Natural Pressure Release to release the steam.

8. **Poultry:**

   This button can be used for making chicken and other poultry recipes in the Instant Pot. The default cooking program is 15 minutes but can be adjusted for "More" to High Pressure for 30 minutes or "Less" for High Pressure for 5 minutes. I always make shredded chicken for homemade tacos and burrito bowls. Add about 1 lb. uncooked chicken, ¼ cup of homemade salsa, 1 cup of bone broth, 1 tsp. cumin, 1 clove garlic minced, ½ tsp oregano, ½ onion, and $1/8$ tsp. paprika into the bottom of your Instant Pot. Secure the lid in place and select the "Poultry" button to the default at High Pressure for 15 minutes. When the cooking cycle has finished, do a Natural Pressure Release for 10 minutes. Carefully open the lid, shred the chicken the two forks, add pepper and salt to taste.

9. **Rice:**

   This button is used to cook rice in your Instant Pot using half the time a conventional rice cooker could use. It uses about 4 to 8 minutes, short grain, Jasmine, White rice, and Basmati rice can all be cooked using this function. You'll need a 1:1 ratio of rice to water (Basmati is a 1:1.5 ratio). It depends on the quantity of food you want to cook on low pressure, when you press the "Rice" button, the cooking duration automatically adjusts. It's always necessary to add further 10-12 minutes to the cooking time to allow the Instant Pot to come to pressure but cooking rice in the "Manual" mode at high pressure is my frequent selection. I usually add 1:1 ratio of rice to water into the bottom of my Instant Pot and set to 3 minutes with a 12 minutes Natural Pressure Release when the timer beeps.

10. **Soup:**

Soup, stock, and broth can be made using the "Soup" button. Water doesn't heavily boil because Instant Pot will control the pressure and temperature so that the liquid doesn't heavily boil. You can adjust the cooking time as required, usually between 20-40 minutes, and the pressure to either Low or High Pressure. Anytime you wish to make homemade bone broth faster than the conventional slow cooker, it is very simple. Click the "Soup" button, set the Low Pressure, and set the cooking time to 120 minutes. Once the timer beeps, do Natural Pressure Release to release the steam.

11. **Steam:**

This button can be used to steam vegetables, seafood or reheat food. Always use the steam rack of your Instant Pot when steaming veggies to avoid burning and sticking to the bottom of your Instant Pot. Add 1-2 cups of water to the inner liner, place the steam rack inside the inner pot and with a stainless steel steam basket on top. Add the vegetables, seafood, etc. in the basket. Select the "Steam" button and then adjust the time using the "+" or "-" key. When you are cooking foods like frozen corn on the cob or a fresh fish filet, adjust the time to 3-5 minutes and 8-10 minutes if you are cooking fresh artichokes could take 9-11 minutes.

12. **Keep Warm Button:**

This button is used to keep food hot when the Instant Pot is done with cooking or to cancel the pressure cooking mode. Immediately cooking time is finished, the Instant Pot will beep and automatically go into the "Keep Warm" function. It will display an "L" in front of a number to indicate how long it's been warm – e.g. "L0:30" for 30 minutes. This button helps to keep food warm (145 to 172°F) for up to 99 hours, 50 minutes.

13. **Cancel Button:**

If by mistake you selected wrong cooking time and you want to stop cooking or adjust pressure cooking time, you can cancel and return to standby mode by selecting the "Keep Warm" / "Cancel" button.

14. **Timer Button**

This button can be used to delay the cooking start time for the Instant Pot for both pressure cooking and slow cook options. Press the Timer button with 10 seconds of pressing Pressure / Manual button or Slow Cook button. To adjust the delayed hours, Use "+/-" buttons then wait a second and press Timer again to set delayed minutes. Press the Keep Warm / Cancel button to cancel the Timer anytime.

Steps to Effectively Clean Your Instant Pot

Step 1: Unplug

Before you start cleaning your Instant Pot, make sure it is unplugged. It's advisable to unplug your Instant Pot whenever it's not in use. For this purpose, you have to make sure it's unplugged for the intensive cleaning you're about to do, for the safety of your Instant Pot and for your safety too.

Step 2: Cleaning housing unit

The outside housing unit cannot go into the dishwasher so you should be able to clean it thoroughly with a rag. Get the rag good and damp with water and cleaning solution, and wipe down both the interior and exterior parts of the main housing unit. To have a perfect cleaning, a sponge is recommended to get those hard or stiff food bits and mineral deposits. Don't fail to clean everywhere you may have tiny particles.

Step 3: Wash the lid

The lid has to be washed properly. This can be done by washing it in the sink with warm water with a little dish soap to make all the residuals are removed because this can contaminate. Some people used a vinegar solution to remove the unpleasant smell from residuals.

Step 4: Check other crevices

There are some parts in the Instant Pot that you might not like to cleaning all the time you are washing the Instant Pot. Get all those crevices and small parts where food residue may build up for some period of time. Remove the Quick Release handle, and wash it with warm-soapy water. In some cases, the steam valve can get blocked if too much deposit builds up there. Remove the shield, located inside the lid which blocks the valve. The shield could pop off easily depending on the model your Instant Pot. Wash the shield in the sink. Check the condensation collection cup at the side of your Instant Pot. It might have collected food residue over time. If it has some residue on it, clean it in the sink.

Step 5: clean sealing ring

The silicone ring found on the underside of the lid will likely need a thorough cleaning. This is what indicates your Instant Pot has a tight seal, and it's an easy spot for food particles or residual smells to lurk. Check it for any signs of damage, as silicone can start to crack over time. If you notice any crack in the silicone ring, it has been damaged and needs a replacement immediately. The silicone ring is dishwasher-safe, so you can pop it in there on the top rack. Once it's thoroughly cleaned, place it back on the underside of the lid, and make sure you've got a secure fit.

Step 6: Wash the inner pot

The inner pot is dishwasher-safe. With this fact, you should be washing the inner pot at regularly intervals. Since you're doing a deep clean, it doesn't hurt to pop the inner pot into the dishwasher together with any of the other dishwasher-safe parts you use with your Instant Pot, such as silicone molds and wire racks. When you finished washing the inner pot, dry it off using a paper towel or use some household vinegar to give it a thorough wipe-down. By doing this, it can get rid of any accumulated residue from things like minerals in your water, or dish detergent. This will make your Instant Pot looks shiny and nice.

Step 7: Steam clean and let dry

At this stage, you have done a thorough cleaning, reassemble all the parts. Don't forget about those small parts like the sealing ring and shield because they can be missed easily. The purpose of this washing and cleaning is to ensure your Instant Pot is safe so you can use it for a long period of time. However, after doing all the washing and cleaning but you realized the sealing ring still has a strange food smell, you may need to deodorize the part with a vinegar steam clean. The process is simple and can be done directly in the Instant Pot by adding a cup of water, a cup of vinegar, and some lemon peels (for extra freshness!) to the inner pot, press "Steam" button and set for a few minutes. When the timer beeps, do a natural pressure release. Open the lid, remove the sealing ring and dry it at a convenient place.

INSTANT POT BREAKFAST RECIPES

Breakfast Porridge

Preparation time: 5 minutes

Cook time: 15 minutes

Total time: 20 minutes

Servings: 1-2

Ingredients:

- 2-3 tablespoons of lightly toasted sunflower seeds or 1 tablespoon of tahini, for seed substitute, use more 2 tablespoons of coconut flakes or coconut butter (grounded)
- 2 tablespoons of unsweetened shredded coconut
- 1 tablespoon of chia seed or flaxseed or substitute with 1 tablespoon of collagen/gelatin powder)
- ½ teaspoon of cinnamon
- 1 teaspoon of ginger, ground
- Dash of turmeric, ground
- Dash of sea salt
- ½ cup of water or coconut milk
- 1 cup of squash, peeled and chopped into large pieces, cooked
- More coconut oil or ghee and water
- Optional hemp protein or collagen
- Pure maple syrup or raw honey
- Extra toppings: tart cherries (pitted), blueberries, pomegranate seeds, sesame seed, and/or coconut cream or yogurt to top.

Cooking Instructions:

1. Add the chopped squash into the bottom of your Instant Pot along with 1 tablespoon of coconut oil.

2. Add in a pinch of cinnamon and nutmeg and cook for about 5 minutes, stirring the squash. Pour 1/3 cup of water into the pot when your squash has coated.

3. Close and lock the lid in place and ensure that the valve is in sealing position. Select Manual, High Pressure for 5 minutes.

4. When the timer beeps, do a natural pressure release for about 10 minutes. Carefully open the lid and drain the water. Puree the squash with a hand blender.

5. Add in your remaining ingredients like dry mix and tahini/sesame mix. Add a splash of milk and give everything a good stir.

6. Close and lock the lid in place. Keep it on warm mode until ready to serve.

7. Serve and enjoy!

Instant Pot Congee

Preparation time: 5 minutes

Cook time: 15 minutes

Total time: 20 minutes

Servings: 6

Ingredients:

- 1 cup of uncooked Jasmine rice
- 6 cups of chicken broth
- 2 chicken breasts or 4 boneless skinless thighs, about 1.5 pounds (680 g)
- 2 tsp. of ginger, grated
- ½ tsp. of fine sea salt
- 4 cups of baby spinach or 2 cups of frozen spinach
- 2 tsp. of toasted sesame oil
- 2 green onions, chopped
- Optional Toppings: Boiled or fried eggs, Sriracha sauce, Chinese pickles or fermented tofu, crushed roasted peanuts or roasted sesame seeds and chopped cilantro.

Cooking Instructions:

1. In a large bowl, add the jasmine rice and pour enough water to cover. Rinse the rice with your hands for several times and then, drain the water. Repeat 2 times.

2. Place the drained rice into the bottom of your Instant pot. Add the chicken broth, chicken, and ginger. Close and lock the lid in place.

3. Select Manual, High Pressure for 15 minutes. When the timer beeps, do a natural pressure release for about 10 minutes.

4. Carefully open the lid and transfer the chicken breasts to a chopping board. Shred the chicken with forks. Add the chicken back into the pot.

5. Press the Sauté button. Add the spinach into the pot and sauté, stirring for about 1 minute. Press the Cancel function. Add the toasted sesame oil and green onion.

6. Give everything a good stir to combine. Scoop the congee into individual bowls and garnish with your desired toppings.

7. Serve and enjoy!

Apple Cinnamon Steel Cut Oats

Preparation time: 5 minutes

Cook time: 25 minutes

Total time: 30 minutes

Servings: 4

Ingredients:

- 2 cups of steel cut oats
- 4 ½ cups of water or non-dairy milk
- 2 medium apples, diced
- 2 tsp. of brown sugar (optional)
- 2 tsp. of cinnamon
- 2 cinnamon sticks
- ¼ tsp. of nutmeg

Cooking Instructions:

1. Add all the ingredients into the bottom of your Instant Pot.

2. Give everything a good stir to combine. Close and lock the lid in place and ensure that the valve is in sealing position.

3. Select Manual, High Pressure for 4 minutes. When the timer beeps, do a natural pressure release for about 15 minutes.

4. Carefully open the lid and stir the oatmeal. Top with more cinnamon and diced apple.

5. Add a splash of milk if you desired a looser oatmeal.

6. Serve immediately and enjoy!

Breakfast Burritos

Preparation time: 15 minutes

Cook time: 30 minutes

Total time: 55 minutes

Servings: 4 - 6

Ingredients:

The Egg Base:

- 8 eggs
- ½ cup of Half and Half
- ½ teaspoon of coarse salt or ¼ teaspoon of table salt
- ¼ teaspoon of pepper
- ½ teaspoon of garlic powder
- 2 tablespoons of chives, chopped
- ¼ cup of onion, diced
- 1 cup of ham, cooked, cubed or ¾ cup of sausage or bacon
- ¾ cup of cheese, shredded, (We used sharp cheddar)
- ½ cup of red bell pepper, diced
- 1 cup of potato, diced
- Flour Tortillas (your desired size for burritos)

Cooking Instructions:

1. Add 1 ½ cups of water into the bottom of your Instant Pot. Spray the pan that will fit into your pot with cooking spray.

2. In a medium bowl, add the eggs and half and half and give everything a good whisk. Add the rest of the ingredients and give everything a good stir.

3. Pour the mixture into the pan and cover it tightly with foil. Place the pan on the trivet and gently place it into the Instant Pot. Close and lock the lid in place.

4. Select Manual, High Pressure for 30 minutes. When the timer beeps, do a quick pressure release. Carefully open the lid and remove the pan. Remove the foil.

5. Use either a spatula or spoon to gently stir and break up the mixture for making the breakfast burritos.

6. Serve and enjoy!

Strawberry Trail Mix Oatmeal

Preparation time: 5 minutes

Cook time: 10 minutes

Total time: 15 minutes

Servings: 2

Ingredients:

- 1 cup of steel cut oats
- 1.5 cups of water
- 2 tablespoons of butter
- 1 cup of freshly squeezed orange juice
- 1 tablespoon of dried cranberries
- 1 tablespoon of raisins
- 1 tablespoon of chopped dried apricots
- 2 tablespoons of pure maple syrup
- ¼ teaspoon of ground cinnamon ☐ 2 tablespoons of chopped pecans
- 1/8 teaspoon of salt
- Toppings: ½ - 1 cup of chopped strawberries, extra cinnamon, extra pecans, any additional fruit or sweetener, milk or almond milk for drizzling on top, granola

Cooking Instructions:

1. Spray the Instant Pot's stainless steel liner with coconut or avocado oil. Press the Sauté function and add the butter to melt.

2. Add all the remaining ingredients into your Instant Pot except for toppings and give everything a good stir to combine.

3. Close and lock the lid in place and ensure that the valve is in sealing position. Select Manual, High Pressure for 10 minutes.

4. When the timer beeps, do a quick pressure release. Carefully open the lid and stir the oatmeal. Ladle the cooked oats into individual bowls and add your desired toppings.

5. Add some extra cinnamon and pecans, a drizzle of almond milk, and a boatload of strawberries, if desired.

6. Serve immediately and enjoy!

Cinnamon Roll French Toast Casserole

Preparation time: 15 minutes

Cook time: 25 minutes

Total time: 40 minutes

Servings: 8

Ingredients:

French Toast Ingredients:

- 1 loaf (12 slices) sourdough bread, sliced into 1-inch cubes (6 cups)
- 8 medium eggs
- 1 cup of milk
- 1 tsp. of vanilla extract
- 2 tbsp. of maple syrup
- ½ cups of walnuts, chopped

Almond Butter Cinnamon Drizzle:

- 2/3 cup of almond butter, drippy
- 2 tbsp. of maple syrup
- 3 tsp. of ground cinnamon
- 1 tbsp. of melted coconut oil

Optional Topping:

- 4 tbsp. of butter, chilled
- ¼ cup of brown sugar

Cooking Instructions:

1. Spray an 8-inch glass bowl with coconut oil cooking spray and set aside. In a medium bowl, mix together all almond butter cinnamon drizzle ingredients.

2. Add more melted coconut oil to the mixture to make the consistency drippy. In another bowl, whisk together the eggs, milk, vanilla, and maple syrup.

3. Add half of the bread cubes and half of the walnuts into the 8-inch glass bowl. Then, drizzle on half of the almond butter cinnamon drizzle over bread mixture.

4. Add the remaining bread cubes and sprinkle on the remaining walnuts and cinnamon drizzle over the bread. Pour egg mixture over the content and mix together the bread cubes with the egg mixture.

5. Sprinkle on the optional topping, if desired. Place metal trivet into the bottom of your Instant Pot and add 1 cup of water. Add the French toast bowl on top of the trivet.

6. Close and lock the lid in place and ensure that the valve is in sealing position. Select Manual, High Pressure for 25 minutes.

7. When the timer beeps, do a quick pressure release. Carefully open the lid and allow to cool for a couple of minutes.

8. Serve with fruit and maple syrup.

Quinoa Breakfast Bowls

Preparation time: 25 minutes

Cook time: 1 minutes

Total time: 25 minutes

Servings: 4

Ingredients:

Quinoa:

- 1 ½ cups of quinoa, soaked in water about 1 hour
- 1 (15 oz.) can of coconut milk or your desired milk
- 1 ½ cups of water
- 1 tsp. of ground cinnamon
- ¼ cup of pure maple syrup
- 2 tsp. of vanilla extract
- ¼ tsp. of salt
- Optional toppings: Fresh fruit, Coconut flakes, Hemp hearts, Non-dairy milk etc

Cooking Instructions:

1. Rinse the quinoa and drain the soaked quinoa. Add the quinoa into your Instant Pot.

2. Add the coconut milk, water, cinnamon, maple syrup, vanilla and salt. Close and lock the lid in place and ensure that the valve is in sealing position.

3. Select the Rice function to cook for 12 minutes. When the timer beeps, do a natural pressure release for about 10 minutes.

4. Carefully open the lid and divide the quinoa into 6 individual containers with lids. Refrigerate them for a couple of hours until ready to serve.

5. When you're ready to serve, top with non-dairy milk, fresh fruit, coconut flakes, hemp hearts, if desired and enjoy!

Tempeh Breakfast Bowl

Serving: 4

Preparation time: 10 minutes

Cook time: 10 minutes

Total time: 20 minutes

Ingredients:

Potato Layer:

- 1 28 ounces bag new or baby Potatoes, cut into quarters

Tempeh Layer:

- ¼ cup of water
- 2 tbsp. of maple syrup
- 2 tsp. of soy sauce
- 1 tsp. of Sriracha, or your desired hot sauce
- 1 8 ounces package tempeh, cut into small cubes

Kale Layer:

- 4 cups of chopped kale
- 2 tbsp. of nutritional yeast
- 1 tbsp. of water
- 1 tsp. of minced garlic

Potato Seasoning:

- 1 tsp. of smoked paprika
- Salt and pepper, to taste

Cooking Instructions:

For the Potato Layer:

1. Pour 1½ cups of water into the bottom of your Instant Pot. Add the vegetable steamer and place the potatoes.

For the Tempeh Layer:

2. In a short Pyrex pan, add all the tempeh ingredients and toss everything to coat. Cover them with a piece of foil and add on the potatoes.

For the Kale Layer:

3. In a medium bowl, mix together the kale, nutritional yeast, water and garlic. Transfer the mixture to the short Pyrex pan and cover them with a piece of foil.

4. Add them on top of the dish containing the tempeh. Place them into the bottom of your Instant Pot. Close and lock the lid in place.

5. Select Manual, High Pressure for 10 minutes. When the timer beeps, do a natural pressure release for about 15 minutes. Carefully open the lid and remove the pans.

For the Potato Seasoning:

6. In a large bowl, add the potatoes along with the paprika. Season with salt and pepper to taste.

7. Serve and enjoy!

Blueberry Oatmeal

Preparation time: 5 minutes

Cook time: 30 minutes

Total time: 35 minutes

Servings: 6

Ingredients:

- 2 ¼ cups of whole oats
- ½ cup of brown sugar
- 14 oz. of canned coconut milk
- 3 cups of water
- 1 cup of blueberries, frozen or fresh
- 1 tsp. of vanilla
- 1/8 tsp. of salt
- ¼ cup of gluten free flour blend

Cooking Instructions:

1. Pour all the ingredients into the bottom of your Instant Pot.

2. Close and lock the lid in place. Select the Bake function to cook for 30 minutes. When the timer beeps, do a quick pressure release.

3. Carefully open the lid and place on a serving bowl.

4. Serve warm and enjoy!

Buckwheat Porridge

Preparation time: 5 minutes

Cook time: 25 minutes

Total time: 30 minutes

Servings: 4

Ingredients:

- 1 cup of raw buckwheat groats
- 3 cups of rice milk
- 1 banana, sliced
- ¼ cup of raisins
- 1 teaspoon of ground cinnamon
- ½ teaspoon of vanilla
- Chopped nuts, optional

Cooking Instructions:

1. Rinse and drain the buckwheat.

2. Add them into the bottom of your Instant Pot. Add the rice milk, banana, raisins, cinnamon and vanilla.

3. Close and lock the lid in place and ensure that the valve is in sealing position. Select Manual, High Pressure for 6 minutes.

4. When the timer beeps, do a natural pressure release for about 20 minutes. Carefully remove the lid and stir everything a good stir.

5. Add additional rice milk to individual servings until your desired consistency is achieved. Sprinkle with chopped nuts if desired.

6. Serve and enjoy!

Mexican Breakfast Casserole

Preparation time: 5 minutes

Cook time: 15 minutes

Total time: 20 minutes

Servings: 4

Ingredients:

- 1 tbsp. of olive oil
- ½ lb. of pork sausage or turkey sausage
- ½ cup of diced yellow onion
- ½ cup of diced red bell pepper
- 2 cloves garlic, minced
- 1 medium sweet potato (shredded or cubed) about 2 cups
- 6 large eggs
- ½ tsp. of chili powder
- A pinch of cayenne pepper
- Sea salt and ground pepper (to taste) ▢ 1 cup of water
- 1 tbsp. of coconut oil, ghee, or butter

Cooking Instructions:

1. Press the Sauté function on your Instant Pot and add the oil.

2. Add the sausage and cook, breaking them apart with a wooden spoon. Add the onion, sweet potato, and peppers, sauté for about 3 minutes.

3. Add the garlic and sauté for additional 1 minute. Grease a 7-cup baking dish with oil and add the potato mixture. Press the Cancel function.

4. In a medium bowl, whisk together the eggs, salt, pepper, and chili powder. Pour the egg mixture over the potato/sausage mixture in the greased 7-cup baking dish.

5. Pour 1 cup of water into the bottom of your Instant Pot and place the trivet. Add the casserole in the Instant Pot.

6. Close and lock the lid in place and ensure that the valve is in sealing position. Select Manual, High Pressure to cook for 5 minutes.

7. When the timer beeps, do a natural pressure release for about 10 minutes. Carefully open the lid and remove the casserole from the Instant Pot.

8. Garnish with Pico de Gallo or Salsa, diced avocado, chopped cilantro, and cheese if desired. Slice and add into individual serving plate.

9. Serve and enjoy!

Cinnamon Crunch Oatmeal

Preparation time: 2 minutes

Cook time: 2 minutes

Total time: 4 minutes

Servings: 4

Ingredients:

- 1 large head of cauliflower or 4 cups of riced cauliflower
- 2 cups of almond milk or your desired dairy-free milk
- 6 tablespoons of coconut sugar or ¼ cup of maple syrup
- 2 teaspoons of cinnamon powder
- ½ teaspoon of nutmeg
- 1 teaspoon of pure vanilla extract
- 2 tablespoons of tapioca starch
- 1 cup of toasted nuts and/or seeds
- Optional toppings: sliced fresh fruits, dried fruits, toasted coconut chips, cacao nibs, chocolate chips, nut butter, etc.

Cooking Instructions:

1. Remove the leaves off the cauliflower and cut off the florets.

2. Grate the cauliflower into the size of rice with a cheese grater or a food processor.

3. Add almond milk, coconut sugar, cinnamon, nutmeg, and vanilla extract into the bottom of your Instant Pot and give everything a good stir.

4. Add the rice sized cauliflower on top of the liquid. Close and lock the lid in place and ensure that the valve is in sealing position.

5. Select Manual, High Pressure for 2 minutes. When the timer beeps, do a quick pressure release.

6. Carefully open the lid and sprinkle tapioca starch over the oatmeal. Give everything a good stir until thickened.

7. Add more tapioca starch if you desire the texture to be thicker. Transfer to serving plates and top with nut, seeds, and/or your desired toppings.

8. Serve warm and enjoy!

Breakfast Potatoes

Servings: 5

Preparation time: 20 minutes

Cook time: 15 minutes

Total time: 35 minutes

Ingredients:

- 6 Yukon gold or red potatoes, or 4 russets (roughly 2 pounds), diced into 1/2-inch cubes
- 2-3 tbsp. of coconut oil
- ¾ cup of water or vegetable broth

Seasonings:

- 1 tbsp. of nutritional yeast
- 2 tsp. of garlic powder ☐ 1 tsp. of onion powder
- ¼ tsp. of paprika
- ¾ tsp. of Himalayan pink salt
- Pepper to taste

Veggies:

- Coconut oil
- 1 medium onion, diced
- 1 green bell pepper

Cooking Instructions:

1. In a medium bowl, combine together the seasonings and set aside.

2. Pat the cubed potatoes dry with a paper towels to drain any excess moisture. Add the potatoes and oil into the bottom of your Instant Pot.

3. Select the Sauté setting and cook the potatoes for about 5 minutes or until they start to change texture.

4. In a medium bowl, mix in the seasonings. Press the Cancel function immediately the potatoes starts to change texture.

5. Pour in the water or broth into the bottom of your Instant Pot but don't mix. Close and lock the lid in place and ensure that the valve is in sealing position.

6. Select Low Pressure to cook for 1 minute. When the timer beeps, do a quick pressure release.

7. Gently mix the potatoes while scraping up any browned bits stuck to the bottom of the pot. Allow them to cool for a couple of minutes. Refrigerate for least 2 hours.

8. Serve and enjoy!

Lemon Blueberry Breakfast Cake

Preparation time: 20 minutes

Cook time: 30 minutes

Total time: 60 minutes

Servings: 2

Ingredients:

- 2 cups of unbleached all-purpose flour
- 2 tsp. of baking powder
- ½ tsp. of salt
- 1 lemon, zest
- ½ cup of unsalted butter, room temp
- ¾ cup of sugar
- 1 egg, room temp
- 1 tsp. of vanilla extract
- ½ cup of buttermilk or any milk with 1 tbsp. of lemon juice
- 2 cups of fresh or frozen blueberries
- ½ lemon, juice (optional)
- ½ cup of powdered sugar (optional)

Cooking Instructions:

1. Grease and flour a dish that will fit into your Instant Pot.

2. In a medium bowl, mix together the flour, baking powder, and salt. Set 2 tbsp. aside.

3. Add zest, sugar, and room temperature butter to mixer and beat everything to combine. Add the egg and vanilla to mixer and mix everything to combine.

4. Working 1 cup at a time, add together the flour mixture and buttermilk to the sugared butter. Incorporate the mixture and add another cup 1 at a time.

5. Lift out the mixer bowl and toss the blueberries with remaining flour and gently fold into batter.

6. Add 2/3 cup of water into the bottom of your Instant Pot with rack. Ladle half of batter into greased dish and place into the Instant Pot.

7. Close and lock the lid in place and ensure that the valve is in sealing position. Select Manual, High Pressure for 30 minutes.

8. When the timer beeps, do a quick pressure release. Carefully open the lid and remove the cake.

9. Allow to cool for a couple of minutes before transferring to a serving bowl. Mix together the juice from ½ a lemon with ½ cup of powdered sugar.

10. Pour the mixture over cake if desired.

11. Serve and enjoy!

Cinnamon Banana Oatmeal

Preparation time: 20 minutes

Cook time: 5 minutes

Total time: 25 minutes

Servings: 3

Ingredients:

- 1 cup of old fashioned oatmeal
- 1 cup of milk
- 1 cup of water
- 2 bananas, slice only 1 banana
- 2 teaspoons of cinnamon
- 1 tablespoon of brown sugar

Cooking Instructions:

1. Lightly spray the bottom of your Instant Pot with non-stick cooking spray. Pour the water, milk and add the oatmeal.

2. Add in the sliced banana, cinnamon and brown sugar. Give everything a good stir. Close and lock the lid in place and ensure that the valve is in sealing position.

3. Select Manual, High Pressure for 5 minutes. When the timer beeps, do a natural pressure release for about 10 minutes, then quick release any remaining pressure.

4. Carefully open the lid stir the oatmeal. Ladle into individual bowls. Slice the second banana and add fresh slices to the top of each bowl.

5. Serve immediately and enjoy!

INSTANT POT SOUP & STEW RECIPES

French Onion Soup

Yield: 4

Preparation time: 5 minutes

Cook time: 15 minutes

Total time: 20 minutes

Ingredients:

- 4 medium onions, sliced
- 3 tbsp. of butter
- 1 tbsp. of olive oil
- 5 cups of vegetable stock
- 2 bay leaves
- 1 tsp. of dried thyme
- 1 tsp. of salt
- 1 tsp. of black pepper
- 4 thick slices of French bread
- 4 slices of Gruyere cheese

Cooking Instructions:

1. Press the Sauté function and add the butter to melt. Add the olive oil and onions. Cook the onions, stirring frequently until they begin to turn brown.

2. Add the vegetable stock, bay leaves, thyme, salt and pepper. Close and lock the lid in place and ensure that the valve is in sealing position.

3. Select Manual, High Pressure for 10 minutes. When the timer beeps, do a natural pressure release for about 15 minutes. Carefully open the lid.

4. Toast the French bread slices with oven broiler. Spray oven-proof bowl with nonstick spray and place a slice of French bread toast.

5. Add the soup on top of bread. Add Gruyere cheese. Place in a broiler and broil until cheese is browned and melted.

6. Serve and enjoy!

Spicy Ethiopian Stew

Servings: 6

Preparation time: 10 minutes

Cook time: 15 minutes

Total time: 25 minutes

Ingredients:

- 1½ cups of dried lentils
- 3 medium garlic cloves, minced
- 3 tbsp. of tomato paste
- 3-5 tsp. of Berbere Spice
- 5 cups of vegetable broth
- 1 yellow onion, chopped
- 2 ½ cups of butternut squash, cut into chunks
- ½ tsp. of sea salt
- ½ tbsp. of maple syrup
- 2 tbsp. of pureed ginger
- ½ (10 oz.) bag chopped frozen spinach

Cooking Instructions:

1. Add all the ingredients into the bottom of your Instant Pot.

2. Close and lock the lid in place and ensure that the valve is in sealing position.

3. Select Manual, High Pressure for 15 minutes. When the timer beeps, do a natural pressure release for about 10 minutes

4. Carefully open the lid.

5. Serve and enjoy!

Cheeseburger Soup

Preparation time: 5 minutes

Cook time: 30 minutes

Total time: 35 minutes

Ingredients:

- 1 lb. of lean ground beef
- ½ cup of shredded carrots
- 2 cups of cubed potatoes
- 16 ounces can of diced tomatoes
- 2 cups of heavy cream
- 16 ounces of cheddar cheese
- 8 ounces of American cheese
- ½ medium onion, diced

Cooking Instructions:

1. Press the Sauté function on your Instant Pot and add the ground beef.

2. Sauté the ground beef until brown and crumbled. Drain grease. Add your chicken broth and veggies.

3. Close and lock the lid in place and ensure that the valve is in sealing position. Select Manual, High Pressure for 30 minutes.

4. When the timer beeps, do a quick pressure release. Carefully open the lid and stir in heavy cream and cheese.

5. Serve and enjoy!

Andouille Sausage Stew

Preparation time: 10 minutes

Cook time: 20 minutes

Total time: 30 minutes

Ingredients:

- 1 lb. of uncooked Pork Andouille Sausage, crumbled
- 1 small onion, halved and thinly sliced
- ½ lb. of grape or cherry tomatoes
- 1 ½ lb. of Yukon Gold potatoes, peeled and cut into 1" pieces
- ¾ lb. of collard greens, stems removed and thinly sliced
- 1 cup of chicken broth
- 1 tsp. of kosher salt
- 20 - 25 turns freshly ground black pepper
- ½ medium lemon, freshly squeezed

Cooking Instructions:

1. Press the Sauté function on your Instant Pot and add the crumbled Andouille sausage.

2. Cook the sausage for about 5 to 8 minutes, stirring occasionally. Add the sliced onions and tomatoes.

3. Give everything a good mix and cook for another 3 to 4 minutes. Add the potatoes, collard greens and broth along with salt and pepper.

4. Close and lock the lid in place and ensure that the valve is in sealing position. Select Manual, High Pressure for 10 minutes.

5. Add the fresh lemon juice. Season with salt and pepper to taste.

6. Serve and enjoy!

Creamed Fennel and Cauliflower Soup

Serves: 4

Preparation time: 10 minutes

Cook time: 5 minutes

Total time: 15 minutes

Ingredients:

For the Salad:

- 1 tbsp. of coconut oil
- 1 white onion, sliced
- 3 cloves garlic, minced
- 1 large or 2 medium sized fennel bulbs, stalks and fronds removed, chopped
- 1 lb. of cauliflower florets, chopped into florets
- 1 cup of coconut milk
- 3 cups of broth (bone broth or vegetable broth)
- 2 tsp. of salt
- Truffle oil, optional for serving
- Black pepper, optional for serving

Cooking Instructions:

1. Press the Sauté function on your Instant Pot and add the coconut oil.

2. Add the onions and sauté until translucent. Add the garlic, fennel, and cauliflower. Cook for about 5 to 10 minutes, until they start to turn golden.

3. Pour the broth and coconut milk. Season with salt to taste. Close and lock the lid in place and ensure that the valve is in sealing position.

4. Select the Soup function to cook for about 15 minutes. When the timer beeps, do a quick pressure release. Carefully open the lid.

5. Puree the soup with a blender to a smooth, creamy consistency. Ladle into individual bowls and drizzle with truffle oil.

6. Top with freshly cracked pepper, and garnish with a left over fennel frond.

7. Serve warm and enjoy!

Pork and Hominy Stew

Preparation time: 10 minutes

Cook time: 50 minutes

Total time: 1 hour

Ingredients:

- 1 ¼ lb. of boneless pork shoulder, trimmed of fat and cut into 4-inch pieces
- Kosher salt
- Fresh cracked pepper
- 1 tbsp. of olive oil, divided
- 1 small white onion, chopped
- 4 garlic cloves, minced
- 2 tbsp. of chili powder
- 4 cups of low sodium chicken broth
- 2 cups of water
- 2 (15 ounces) cans hominy, drained and rinsed
- 4 ounces of diced avocado and lime wedges, for serving
- Cilantro for garnish

Cooking Instructions:

1. Generously season the pork on both sides with salt. Press Sauté function on your Instant Pot and add the olive oil.

2. Add the pork and sauté for about 8 minutes or until they are browned on all sides, and set aside.

3. Add the rest of the oil, onion, garlic, and chili powder and cook for about 4 minutes or until soft.

4. Add the broth and water, cook, stirring to deglaze any browned bits stuck to the bottom of the pot. Add the pork back into the Instant Pot.

5. Close and lock the lid in place and ensure that the valve is in sealing position. Select Manual, High Pressure for 45 minutes.

6. When the timer beeps, do a quick pressure release. Carefully open the lid and drain the fat. Transfer the pork to a chopping board and shred with two forks.

7. Stir in hominy and heat through. Top with avocado and lime and garnish with cilantro. Serve and enjoy!

Swiss Chard Stem Soup

Ingredients:

- 8 cups of Swiss chard stems, diced
- 3 leeks, green and white, diced
- Celeriac, peeled and diced
- Potato, peeled and diced
- 1.5 cups of chicken stock
- 1 cup of coconut milk
- Pinch of salt
- Pepper to taste

Cooking Instructions:

1. Press the Sauté function on your Instant Pot and add 2 tbsp. of oil. Add the leeks and sauté until soft.

2. Add the diced Swiss chard, cooked leeks, celeriac, potato, chicken stock and coconut milk into the pot.

3. Season with salt and pepper. Close and lock the lid in place and ensure that the valve is in sealing position.

4. Select the Soup button and allow it to cook. When the timer beeps, do a quick pressure release. Carefully open the lid.

5. Puree the soup with an immersion blender. Ladle into individual bowls.

6. Serve and enjoy!

Green Chile Stew

Preparation time: 30 minutes

Cook time: 38 minutes

Total time: 1 hour 8 minutes

Servings: 10 bowls

Ingredients:

Meat Ingredients:

- ½ package of Butler Soy Curls rehydrated or Seitan 1 tube GimmeLean Sausage, or 16 ounces of portabella Mushrooms
- 1 teaspoon of chili powder
- 1 teaspoon of ground cumin
- 1 teaspoon of garlic powder
- 1 teaspoon of onion powder

Broth Ingredients:

- 1 yellow onion, diced
- 2 carrots, diced
- 2 stalks celery, diced
- 4-5 cloves garlic
- 2 cups of vegetable broth
- 2 cups of water
- 1 teaspoon of oregano
- 1 cup of dried rinsed, Pinto Beans

Stew Ingredients:

- 3 Yukon gold potatoes, cubed
- 15 ounces can of fire roasted tomatoes
- 24 ounces package of Select new Mexico green Chiles
- ¼ cup of lime juice
- ¼ teaspoon of salt
- ¼ teaspoon of ground pepper

Cooking Instructions:

1. Press the Sauté function on your Instant Pot and add your desired meat. Add the garlic powder, onion powder, chili powder and cumin and stir occasionally until browned.

2. Add some veggie broth to prevent it from sticking. Remove them from pot and place in a bowl. Add the onion, carrots, and celery and sauté until soft and translucent.

3. Deglaze the pot to remove any browned bits from sticking to the bottom of the pot. Add the minced garlic and stir for 1 minute.

4. Press the Cancel function. Add the veggie broth, water, oregano, and dried beans. Close and lock the lid in place and ensure that the valve is in sealing position.

5. Select Manual, High Pressure for 30 minutes. When the timer beeps, do a natural pressure release for about 10 minutes, then quick release any remaining pressure.

6. Carefully remove the lid and stir broth and add potatoes, chilies, tomatoes, and your desired meat. Close and lock the lid in place.

7. Select Manual, High Pressure for 8 minutes. When the timer beeps, do a natural pressure release for about 5 minutes, then quick release any remaining pressure.

8. Carefully remove the lid and stir in lime juice. Stir in masa flour, 1 tablespoon at a time until your desired thickness is achieved.

9. Serve and enjoy!

Butternut Cauliflower Soup

Preparation time: 5 minutes

Cook time: 25 minutes

Total time: 30 minutes

Servings: 6 cups

Ingredients:

- 1 onion, diced
- 1 - 2 teaspoon of oil
- 2 - 3 cloves garlic, minced
- 1 pound of frozen cauliflower
- 1 pound of frozen cubed butternut squash
- 2 cups of vegetable broth (chicken broth)
- 1 teaspoon of paprika
- ½ - 1 teaspoon of dried thyme
- ¼ - ½ teaspoon of red pepper flakes, optional
- ¼ teaspoon of sea salt or more
- ½ cup of half and half, milk, or cream
- Toppings: grated cheddar cheese, crumbled bacon, Sriracha or hot sauce, parmesan and/or Gouda cheese, sour cream cheddar, and chives, chopped green onions, etc.

Cooking Instructions:

1. Press the Sauté function on your Instant Pot and add the oil. Add the onion and cook until tender and golden.

2. Add the garlic, cauliflower, butternut, veggie broth, and spices. Close and lock the lid in place and ensure that the valve is in sealing position.

3. Select Manual, High Pressure for 5 minutes. When the timer beeps, do a quick pressure release. Carefully open the lid and add half and half.

4. Blend the soup with an immersion blender or food processor. Top with your desired toppings.

5. Serve and enjoy!

Italian Beef Stew

Preparation time: 10 minutes

Cook time: 35 minutes

Total time: 45 minutes

Servings: 6-8

Ingredients:

- 3 pounds of beef stew meat OR 2 pounds of ground beef, browned.
- 1 onion, diced
- 4 carrots, sliced
- 8 ounces of fresh baby portabella mushrooms, sliced and optional
- 24 ounces of beef broth
- 15 ounces can of diced tomatoes
- 3 tablespoons of flour
- 1 teaspoon of dried basil leaves
- 1 teaspoon of dried thyme leaves
- 1 teaspoon of salt
- 1 teaspoon of pepper
- Dried parsley

Cooking Instructions:

1. Press the Sauté function on your Instant Pot and add the meat.

2. Add the ground beef if desired. Sauté the ground beef and drain grease. Add the carrots, broth, flour, basil, and thyme.

3. Season with salt and pepper. Add the diced tomatoes into the bottom of your Instant Pot and give everything a good stir.

4. Close and lock the lid in place and ensure that the valve is in sealing position. Select Manual, High Pressure for 35 minutes.

5. When the timer beeps, do a quick pressure release. Carefully open the lid and stir in mushrooms. Give everything a good stir.

6. Serve and enjoy!

Cheddar Broccoli Potato Soup

Servings: 4-6

Preparation time: 10 minutes

Cook time: 15 minutes

Total time: 25 minutes

Ingredients:

- 2 tablespoons of butter
- 2 cloves garlic, crushed
- 1 small sized broccoli head, broken into large florets
- 2 pounds of Yukon Gold Potatoes, peeled and cut into small chunks
- 4 cups of vegetable or chicken broth
- Pinch of salt
- Pepper to taste
- 1 cup of half and half
- 1 cup of shredded cheddar cheese
- 6 slices of bacon, optional
- Chopped green onion or chives for garnish

Cooking Instructions:

1. Press the Sauté button on your Instant Pot and add the butter to melt. Add the crushed garlic and cook for about 1 minute or until garlic starts to brown.

2. Add the broccoli, potatoes, and broth. Season with salt and pepper. Close and lock the lid in place and ensure that the valve is in sealing position.

3. Select Manual, High Pressure for 5 minutes. When the timer beeps, do a natural pressure release for about 10 minutes, then quick release any remaining pressure.

4. Carefully open the lid. If using bacon, microwave or cook the bacon until your desired crispiness is achieved and reserve aside.

5. Add the half and half and ½ cup of cheddar cheese into the pot. Puree the soup with an immersion blender until smooth. Season with more salt and pepper.

6. Ladle into individual bowls and top with remaining cheddar and bacon if desired. Serve warm and enjoy!

Spicy Beef Stew

Preparation time: 5 minutes

Cook time: 40 minutes

Total time: 45 minutes

Ingredients:

- 2 tablespoons of ghee or avocado oil
- 1 pound of beef stew meat, cut into cubes
- 1 onion, diced
- 3 medium potatoes, chopped
- 4 carrots, chopped
- 2 celery stalks, chopped
- 2 cups of kale leaves, stems removed
- 1 teaspoon of garlic powder
- ½ teaspoon of black pepper
- 2 cups of bone broth
- 2 tablespoons of your desired hot sauce
- Sea salt, to taste

Cooking Instructions:

1. Press the Sauté function on your Instant Pot and add the avocado oil.

2. Add the meat and cook, stir frequently until the meat is browned. Add the remaining ingredient, except salt and give everything a good stir.

3. Close and lock the lid in place and ensure that the valve is in sealing position. Select the Meat/Stew to cook for about 40 minutes.

4. When the timer beeps, do a quick pressure release. Carefully open the lid and season with salt.

5. Serve and enjoy!

Stuffed Pepper Soup

Serves: 6

Preparation time: 5 minutes

Cook time: 25 minutes

Total time: 30 minutes

Ingredients:

- 1 tablespoon of extra virgin olive oil
- 3-4 cloves garlic, minced
- ½ onion, thinly sliced
- ½ can of tomato paste
- 1 teaspoon of cumin
- 1 teaspoon of chili powder
- 1 teaspoon of black pepper
- 1 teaspoon of salt
- 2 bell peppers, sliced or diced
- ½ - 1 pound of ground beef, uncooked
- 12 ounces can of diced tomatoes
- 5 cups of beef broth
- 1 cup of organic brown rice, uncooked
- 3 tablespoons of cornmeal
- Parmesan cheese, for garnish
- Green onions, for garnish

Cooking Instructions:

1. Press the Sauté function on your Instant Pot and add the ground beef. Add the garlic and onions.

2. Sauté the ingredients until ground beef is cooked through and onions are soft. Press the Cancel function.

3. Add the tomato paste, cumin, black pepper and salt along with the peppers, diced tomatoes, and beef broth.

4. Give everything a good mix to combine. Stir in the rice and mix until blended. Close and lock the lid in place and ensure that the valve is in sealing position.

5. Select Manual, High Pressure for 23 minutes. When the timer beeps, do a quick pressure release.

6. Carefully remove the lid and add the cornmeal little by little. Give everything a good stir. Ladle into serving bowls and garnish with parmesan cheese.

7. Serve with fresh dinner rolls or breadsticks and enjoy!

INSTANT POT POULTRY RECIPES

Chicken Noodle Soup

Preparation time: 10 minutes

Cook time: 10 minutes

Total time: 30 minutes

Servings: 4

Ingredients:

- 3 large carrots, peeled and sliced
- 2 ribs celery, sliced
- 1 cup of chopped spinach
- 1 boneless skinless chicken breast chopped (fresh or frozen)
- 1 tsp. of parsley
- 1 tsp. of salt
- ½ tsp. of thyme
- ¼ tsp. of garlic powder
- 1/8 tsp. of black pepper
- 4 cups of low sodium chicken broth
- 1 cup of short pasta such as Ditalini or Orzo
- 1 cup 1% milk
- 2 tbsp. of corn starch

Cooking Instructions:

1. Add the carrots, celery, spinach, chicken, parsley, salt, thyme, garlic powder, black pepper and chicken broth into the bottom of your Instant Pot.

2. Give everything a good stir. Close and lock the lid in place and ensure that the valve is in sealing position.

3. Select Manual, High Pressure for 4 minutes for veggies with more bite, 5 minutes for tender veggies.

4. When the timer beeps, do a quick pressure release. Carefully open the lid and add the pasta. Press the Sauté function and cook for 4-5 minutes until pasta is al dente.

5. In a medium bowl, whisk together the milk and corn starch. Stir in the mixture into the soup to thicken.

6. Serve and enjoy!

Chicken Taco Soup

Preparation time: 5 minutes

Cook time: 30 minutes

Total time: 35 minutes

Serves: 6 - 8

Ingredients:

- 2 large boneless skinless chicken breasts (about 1 pound)
- 1 cup of diced onion
- 1 (15 ounces) can of chicken broth (or 1 ½ cups of water)
- 1 (15 ounces) can kidney beans, undrained
- 1 (15 ounces) can black beans, undrained
- 1 (15 ounces) can corn, undrained
- 1 (15 ounces) can diced tomatoes
- 1 (8 ounces) can tomato sauce
- 2 tablespoons of taco seasoning
- 2 tablespoons of Hidden Valley Ranch Seasoning
- Optional Taco Toppings: Sour cream, Avocado Slices, Pico de Gallo, Diced Green onions, Corn Chips, Sliced Olives, Shredded Cheddar Cheese etc.

Cooking Instructions:

1. Add all the ingredients (except for the optional toppings) into the bottom of your Instant Pot.

2. Give everything a good stir to combine. Close and lock the lid in place and ensure that the valve is in sealing position.

3. Select Manual, High Pressure for 30 minutes. When the timer beeps, do a quick pressure release.

4. Carefully open the lid and transfer the chicken breasts to a bowl. Shred them with two forks.

5. Add the shredded chicken breast back into the pot and give everything a good stir. Serve with your desired toppings and enjoy!

Chicken Cacciatore

Preparation time: 15 minutes

Cook time: 40 minutes

Total time: 55 minutes

Ingredients:

- 4 (6 oz.) bone-in chicken thighs, with skin, rinsed
- 2 tbsp. of olive oil
- 3 stalks celery, chopped
- ½ onion, chopped
- 1 (4 oz.) package sliced fresh mushrooms
- 2 cloves garlic, minced
- 1 (14 oz.) can stewed tomatoes
- 2 tsp. of herbes de Provence
- ¾ cup of water
- 3 cubes of chicken bouillon, crumbled
- 2 tbsp. of tomato paste
- A pinch of red pepper flakes (optional)
- A pinch of ground black pepper to taste (optional)

Cooking Instructions:

1. Pat the chicken thighs dry with paper towels. Press the Sauté function on your Instant Pot and add the oil.

2. Add the chicken and sauté on each side for about 6 minutes or until browned. Remove the chicken to a bowl, reserving drippings in the pot.

3. Add the celery, onion, and mushrooms into the bottom of your Instant Pot. Sauté, stirring frequently until soft, about 5 minutes.

4. Add the garlic and sauté for about 2 minutes or until fragrant. Add the chicken back in the pot. Add the tomatoes and tomato paste.

5. Sprinkle with herbes de Provence. Pour ¾ cup of water and add the bouillon. Close and lock the lid in place and ensure that the valve is in sealing position.

6. Select Manual, High Pressure for 11 minutes. When the timer beeps, do a quick pressure release for about 5 minutes.

7. Carefully open the lid and test the chicken for doneness. The meat thermometer should read 165 degrees F (74 degrees C).

8. Season with red pepper flakes and black pepper.

9. Serve and enjoy!

Chicken Cordon Bleu

Preparation time: 12 minutes

Cook time: 15 minutes

Total time: 27 minutes

Servings: 4

Ingredients:

- 2 cups of panko breadcrumbs
- 1 teaspoon of salt
- ½ teaspoon of pepper
- 3-4 chicken breast, halves boneless, skinless
- 8 slices deli ham, sliced
- 4 slices of Swiss cheese
- ½ cup of butter, melted
- 1 cup of chicken broth

Cooking Instructions:

1. Combine together the Panko, salt, and pepper in a shallow dish and reserve aside. Pound the chicken breast into ½-inch thickness.

2. Add 2 slices of ham over each chicken breast. Add a slice of Swiss cheese over the ham and roll chicken it up.

3. Dredge each of the chicken roll in butter, then dip in breadcrumbs. Add them seam side down into the bottom of your Instant Pot.

4. Pour the rest of the butter over the chicken and add the chicken broth in the cracks between the chicken breasts.

5. Close and lock the lid in place and ensure that the valve is in sealing position. Select Manual, High Pressure for 8 minutes.

6. When the timer beeps, do a natural pressure release for about 5 minutes, then quick release any remaining pressure. Carefully open the lid.

7. Serve and enjoy!

BBQ Chicken with Potatoes

Preparation time: 10 minutes

Cook time: 15 minutes

Total time: 25 minutes

Ingredients:

- 2 lb. of frozen chicken if fresh, adjust cooking time
- 1 cup of your desired BBQ sauce
- ½ cup of water
- 1 tbsp. of Italian seasoning
- 1 tbsp. of minced garlic
- 2-3 large potatoes, chopped
- 1 large red onion, sliced

Cooking Instructions:

1. Add all ingredients into the bottom of your Instant Pot.

2. Close and lock the lid in place and ensure that the valve is in sealing position.

3. Select the Poultry function for 15 minutes for frozen and 12 minutes for fresh chicken.

4. When the timer beeps, do a natural pressure release for about 10 minutes. Carefully open the lid and remove the chicken.

5. Shred the chicken with two forks. Add the shredded chicken back into the pot and toss everything to combine with sauce.

6. Serve and enjoy!

Chicken Chile Verde

Serves: 6

Preparation time: 5 minutes

Cook time: 25 minutes

Total time: 30 minutes

Ingredients:

- 2 pounds of chicken thighs or chicken breasts
- ½ tsp. of ground cumin
- ¼ tsp. of garlic powder
- 16 oz. of salsa verde
- Pinch of salt
- Black pepper, to taste

Cooking Instructions:

1. Add the chicken into the bottom of your Instant Pot.

2. Add the cumin, garlic powder, and salsa verde. Close and lock the lid in place and ensure that the valve is in sealing position.

3. Select Manual, High Pressure for 25 minutes. When the timer beeps, do a quick pressure release.

4. Carefully open the lid and remove the chicken. Shred the chicken with two forks. Add the shredded chicken back into the pot.

5. Season with salt and black pepper, to taste. Give everything a good stir.

6. Serve with tortillas, rice, use in burritos, quesadillas, tacos, salads, etc.

Pineapple Chicken Breasts

Preparation time: 10 minutes

Cook time: 10 minutes

Total time: 30 minutes

Servings: 4

Ingredients:

- 4 boneless skinless chicken breasts
- 1 398ml can pineapple chunks with juice 14 ounces
- 3 tbsp. of sodium-reduced soy sauce
- 3 tbsp. of brown sugar packed
- ½ tsp. of salt
- Pinch of black pepper
- 1 tbsp. of corn starch
- 1 tbsp. of water

Cooking Instructions:

1. Add pineapple chunks with juice, soy sauce, sugar, salt and pepper into the bottom of your Instant Pot.

2. Give everything a good stir to combine and place the chicken breasts on top of the pineapple. Close and lock the lid in place.

3. Select Manual, High Pressure for 10 minutes. When the timer beeps, do a natural pressure release for about 10 minutes, then quick release any remaining pressure.

4. Carefully open the lid. Select the Sauté function and adjust to less heat. In a medium bowl, mix together the corn starch and water.

5. Stir the mixture into the sauce. Sauté and stir until the sauce has thickened. Serve over rice, noodles or with a side of veggies.

Orange Chicken

Servings: 4

Preparation time: 10 minutes

Cook time: 20 minutes

Total time: 30 minutes

Ingredients:

- ½ cup of chicken broth
- ¼ cup of freshly squeezed orange juice
- ½ cup of seasoned rice vinegar
- ½ cup of soy sauce
- 2 tbsp. of honey
- 2 cloves garlic, minced
- 1 tbsp. of grated orange zest, about 1 orange
- 1 tsp. of red pepper flakes
- ¼ tsp. of ground ginger
- ¼ tsp. of black pepper
- 1 ½ lb. uncooked boneless skinless chicken breasts, We used 3 (8 ounces) chicken breasts
- 2 tbsp. of cornstarch
- 2-4 tbsp. of freshly squeezed orange juice
- Green onion, sliced
- Cilantro, chopped
- Sesame seeds
- Cauliflower rice, brown rice, for serving

Cooking Instructions:

1. Spray your Instant Pot with cooking spray. In a medium bowl, whisk together the broth, ¼ cup of orange juice, vinegar, soy sauce and honey.

2. Add the garlic, orange zest, red pepper flakes, ground ginger, and black pepper. Pour half of the mixture into the bottom of your Instant Pot.

3. Add in chicken breasts. Pour the rest of the sauce over chicken breasts. Close and lock the lid in place and ensure that the valve is in sealing position.

4. Select Manual, High Pressure for 12 minutes. When the timer beeps, do a quick pressure release. Carefully open the lid and transfer the chicken to a bowl.

5. Shred the chicken with two forks. In a medium bowl, whisk together the cornstarch with 2-4 tbsp. of orange juice. Stir the mixture into the pot.

6. Press the Sauté function and bring the pot to a boil. Add the chicken back into the pot and give everything a good stir.

7. Simmer for about 5 minutes or until the sauce has thickened. Adjust the seasoning to your desired taste.

8. Garnish with cilantro, sesame seeds and green onion, if desired.

9. Serve and enjoy!

Chicken Marsala

Preparation time: 5 minutes

Cook time: 15 minutes

Total time: 20 minutes

Yield: 4

Ingredients:

- 2 tablespoons of butter
- Flour, for dipping
- 1 - 1.5 lb. of thinly sliced chicken breasts
- 8-12 oz. sliced mushrooms (We used baby portabellas)
- 4 oz. pancetta, finely cubed
- 2/3 cup of marsala cooking wine
- 1 cup of chicken broth
- 2 cloves garlic, minced
- 1 tablespoon of cornstarch + 1 tablespoon of water
- Fresh parsley to garnish

Cooking Instructions:

1. Press the Sauté function on your Instant Pot and add the butter. Dip both sides of the chicken breasts in flour.

2. Add the dredged chicken into the bottom of your Instant Pot. Cook them to brown in the butter for about 1-2 minutes on each side and set aside.

3. Add the garlic, pancetta, mushrooms and Marsala wine and cook for about 2 minutes. Press the Cancel function.

4. Place the chicken breasts into the pot along with chicken broth, nestling chicken down into the mushrooms. Close and lock the lid in place.

5. Select Manual, High Pressure for 8 minutes. When the timer beeps, do a quick pressure release. Carefully open the lid and remove the chicken breasts.

6. Press the Sauté function. In a medium bowl, whisk together the cornstarch and water. Pour the mixture into the pot.

7. Shred the chicken breast and add them back into the pot.

8. Simmer for about 5-10 minutes, stirring or until the sauce thickens.

9. Add the chicken on bowls, spoon mushroom sauce over chicken, garnish with parsley.

10. Serve hot and enjoy!

Honey Garlic Chicken

Preparation time: 5 minutes

Cook time: 20 minutes

Total time: 25 minutes

Servings: 4

Ingredients:

- 1/3 cup of honey
- 4 cloves garlic, minced
- ½ cup of low sodium soy sauce
- ½ cup of no salt ketchup
- ½ tsp. of dried oregano
- 2 tbsp. of chopped fresh parsley
- 1 tbsp. of sesame seed oil
- 4 - 6 bone-in, skinless chicken thighs
- Pinch of salt
- Fresh ground pepper, to taste
- ½ tbsp. of tbsp. toasted sesame seeds, for garnish
- Sliced green onions, for garnish

Cooking Instructions:

1. In a medium bowl, combine together the honey, minced garlic, soy sauce, ketchup, oregano and parsley. Give everything a good mix to combine and set aside.

2. Press the Sauté function on your Instant Pot and add the sesame oil. Generously season the chicken thighs with salt and pepper.

3. Place the chicken thighs into the Instant Pot and sauté for about 2 to 3 minutes per side. Add the prepared honey garlic sauce into the bottom of your Instant Pot.

4. Close and lock the lid in place and ensure that the valve is in sealing position. Select the Poultry function to cook for 20 minutes.

5. When the timer beeps, do a quick pressure release. Press the Cancel function. Carefully open the lid and remove the chicken.

6. Shred the chicken and ladle the sauce over the chicken. Garnish with toasted sesame seeds and green onions.

7. Serve and enjoy!

General Tso's Chicken

Preparation time: 20 minutes

Cook time: 3 minutes

Total time: 23 minutes

Servings: 4

Ingredients:

- 3 lb. of chicken breasts cut into bite size pieces
- 1 cup of potato starch
- 2 eggs
- 2 tbsp. of peanut oil
- 2 tbsp. of natural sesame seeds toasted
- 1 tbsp. of fresh ginger root, minced
- 1 tbsp. of fresh garlic, minced
- ½ cup of chicken stock/broth

Sauce:

- ¼ cup of seasoned rice vinegar
- ¼ cup of light brown sugar
- ¼ cup of Shaoxing wine ☐ ¼ cup of dark soy sauce
- ¼ cup of sweet/black soy sauce
- 1 tsp. of pure sesame oil
- 2 tsp. of sambal Oelek ground chili paste

Rice:

- 3 scallions

Cooking Instructions:

1. Rinse the chicken and pat dry with a paper towel. Add the chicken into Ziploc bag and toss with potato starch to coat.

2. Dredge the chicken into the egg mixture and set aside. Press the Sauté function and add the oil. Shake off any excess egg and add them into your Instant Pot.

3. Sauté the chicken on both sides and transfer to a plate. Add some sesame oil and add the sesame seeds to toast. Add the minced ginger, garlic and cook for 1 minute.

4. Add the chicken broth and sauce mixture to the pot and whisk everything. Press the Cancel function. Add the chicken into sauce.

5. Close and lock the lid in place and ensure that the valve is in sealing position. Select Manual, High Pressure for 3 minutes.

6. When the timer beeps, do a natural pressure release for about 10 minutes. Carefully open the lid and remove the chicken.

7. Shred the chicken and add them back into the pot. Add cut scallions and give everything a good stir. Simmer the sauce for a couple of minutes or until thick.

8. Serve and enjoy!

Chicken Adobo

Serves 4 - 6

Preparation time: 5 minutes

Cook time: 30 minutes

Total time: 35 minutes

Ingredients:

- 10 chicken drumsticks
- Pinch of salt
- Pepper to taste
- 2 tbsp. of avocado oil
- ½ yellow onion, sliced
- 10 to 12 garlic gloves, peeled and chopped
- ½ cup of soy sauce
- ½ cup of distilled white vinegar
- ¼ cup of water
- 3 bay leaves
- 1 ½ tsp. of ground black pepper

Cooking Instructions:

1. Generously season the chicken drumsticks with salt and pepper. Press the Sauté function and add the oil.

2. Sauté the chicken pieces on both sides until browned. Add all the remaining ingredients to the pot.

3. Close and lock the lid in place and ensure that the valve is in sealing position. Select Manual, High Pressure for 9 minutes.

4. When the timer beeps, do a natural pressure release for about 10 minutes. Carefully open the lid and discard the bay leaves. Press the Sauté function.

5. Simmer for 10 to 15 minutes or until sauce thickens. Transfer the chicken to a serving bowl and top with sauce.

6. Serve with rice and enjoy!

Teriyaki Chicken and Rice

Preparation time: 5 minutes

Cook time: 23 minutes

Total time: 43 minutes

Servings: 4

Ingredients:

- 2 ½ cups of low sodium chicken broth
- ¼ cup of hoisin sauce
- 3 tbsp. of low sodium soy sauce
- 2 tbsp. of liquid honey
- 1 tbsp. of white vinegar
- 2 tsp. of minced garlic
- 1 tsp. of minced ginger
- 1 pinch red pepper flakes, optional
- 1 ½ cups of long grain brown rice
- 2 boneless skinless chicken breasts
- 1 red bell pepper, chopped
- 1 large carrot, diced
- 1 cup of frozen peas

Cooking Instructions:

1. Add the broth, soy sauce, hoisin sauce, vinegar, honey, garlic, ginger and pepper flakes if desired into the bottom of your Instant Pot.

2. Give everything a good stir. Add in the rice and place the chicken breasts on top. Close and lock the lid in place and ensure that the valve is in sealing position.

3. Select Manual, High Pressure for 20 minutes. When the timer beeps, do a quick pressure release. Carefully open the lid and add the pepper, carrot and peas.

4. Close and lock the lid in place. Select Manual, High Pressure for 3 minutes. When the timer beeps, do a quick pressure release.

5. Serve warm and enjoy!

Salsa Lime Chicken

Preparation time: 5 minutes

Cook time: 25 minutes

Total time: 30 minutes

Servings: 6

Ingredients:

- 3 chicken breasts
- 16 oz. of salsa
- Juice from 1 large lime

Cooking Instructions:

1. Add the chicken breasts into the bottom of your Instant Pot.

2. Pour salsa over the chicken and pour the juice from 1 lime over the top of the salsa.

3. Close and lock the lid in place and ensure that the valve is in sealing position.

4. Select the Poultry function and set timer for 25 minutes.

5. When the timer beeps, do a quick pressure release. Carefully open the lid and stir.

6. Serve and enjoy!

Honey Mustard Curry Chicken

Preparation time: 5 minutes

Cook time: 30 minutes

Total time: 35 minutes

Servings: 7

Ingredients:

- 1 tbsp. of olive oil
- 4 boneless skinless chicken breasts
- 1 tsp. of dried minced onions
- 4 tbsp. of melted butter
- ½ cup of honey
- ¼ cup of Dijon mustard
- 1 tsp. of sea salt
- 1 ½ tsp. of curry powder
- ½ cup of water

Cooking Instructions:

1. In a medium bowl, whisk together the melted butter, honey, mustard, sea salt and curry powder until blended.

2. Add the olive oil into the bottom of your Instant Pot and add the chicken breasts. Sprinkle with dried minced onions.

3. Add water and pour the honey mustard mixture on the chicken. Close and lock the lid in place and ensure that the valve is in sealing position.

4. Select Manual, High Pressure for 10 minutes. When the timer beeps, do a natural pressure release for about 10 minutes.

5. Carefully open the lid and remove chicken to a bowl. Press the Sauté function and simmer until sauce thickens.

6. Shred the chicken with two forks and pour sauce over chicken.

7. Serve and enjoy!

INSTANT POT BEEF & PORK RECIPES
Pulled Pork Tacos

Preparation time: 10 minutes

Cook time: 30 minutes

Total time: 40 minutes

Servings: 8

Ingredients:

- 1 ½ teaspoon of sea salt
- 1 teaspoon of freshly ground pepper
- ½ teaspoon of garlic powder
- ½ teaspoon of cumin
- ½ teaspoon of chipotle chili powder
- 1 large yellow onion, sliced
- 1 to 4 lb. of pork shoulder, bone in or out
- 1 cup of chicken or beef broth
- Your desired tortillas
- Garnish: sliced purple cabbage and chopped cilantro and lime

Cooking Instructions:

1. In a medium bowl, combine together all spices and give everything a good mix. Add the onions and broth into the bottom of your Instant Pot.

2. Generously season the pork on all sides with spices. Add the pork to Instant Pot. Close and lock the lid in place and ensure that the valve is in sealing position.

3. Select the Meat function for 60 minutes. When the timer beeps, do a natural pressure release for about 10 minutes.

4. Carefully open the lid and transfer the meat to a cutting board, discard liquid and onions. Shred the meat with two forks, and skim the fat.

5. If you desire browned crispy edges, simmer in a hot pan for a couple of minutes. Make tacos and garnish with sliced purple cabbage and chopped cilantro if desired.

6. Serve and enjoy!

Beer-Braised Pulled Ham

Preparation time: 10 minutes

Cook time: 25 minutes

Total time: 35 minutes

Servings: 16

Ingredients:

- 2 bottles (12 oz. each) beer or nonalcoholic beer
- ¾ cup of German or Dijon mustard, divided
- ½ tsp. of coarsely ground pepper
- 1 fully cooked bone-in ham (4 lb.)
- 4 fresh rosemary sprigs
- 16 pretzel hamburger buns, split
- Dill pickle slices, optional

Cooking Instructions:

1. In a medium bowl, whisk together the beer, ½ cup of mustard and pepper and pour the mixture into the bottom of your Instant Pot.

2. Add ham and rosemary. Close and lock the lid in place and ensure that the valve is in sealing position. Select Manual, High Pressure for 20 minutes.

3. When the timer beeps, do a natural pressure release for about 10 minutes, then quick pressure any remaining pressure.

4. Carefully open the lid and remove ham. Remove the rosemary sprigs and drain the fat from liquid remaining in Instant Pot.

5. Press the Sauté function and adjust for high heat. Bring the pot to a boil; cook for 5 minutes. Shred the meat with two forks and remove the bone.

6. Add the ham back to the Instant Pot and heat through. Add the shredded ham on pretzel bun bottoms with rest of the mustard and, dill pickle slices if desired.

7. Serve and enjoy!

Beef Masala Curry

Preparation time: 10 minutes

Cook time: 30 minutes

Total time: 40 minutes

Serves: 4

Ingredients:

- 2 pounds of stewing beef, cut in 2 inch cubes
- 1 medium onion, chopped
- 3 garlic cloves, minced
- ½ cup of crushed tomatoes
- ¼ cup of fresh cilantro, chopped
- 1 teaspoon of salt
- 1 teaspoon of freshly ground black pepper
- 1 teaspoon of turmeric
- 1 tablespoon of garam masala
- ½ teaspoon of cumin
- ½ teaspoon of coriander
- ½ teaspoon of cayenne pepper
- ½ teaspoon of smoked paprika
- ½ teaspoon of lemon zest
- 1 teaspoon of brown sugar
- 1 tablespoon of oil
- 1 cup of beef stock

Cooking Instructions:

1. Press the Sauté function on your Instant Pot and add the oil. Add the chopped onions, garlic, spices, salt and pepper.

2. Sauté the onions for about 3 minutes or until translucent. Stir in the crushed tomatoes, brown sugar and bring the pot to a boil.

3. Add the mixture in a food processor and blend the mixture into a paste. Sauté the meat to brown on both sides.

4. Add the blended spice paste, stock and add lemon zest. Close and lock the lid in place. Select Manual, High Pressure for 30 minutes.

5. When the timer beeps, do a quick pressure release. Carefully open the lid. Serve with steamed rice and chopped cilantro.

Japanese Pork Tender Rib Stew

Preparation time: 10 minutes

Cook time: 60 minutes

Total time: 1 hour 10 minutes

Serves: 2 - 3

Ingredients:

- 820 gm soft pork ribs (aka pork cartilage)
- 4 slices ginger
- 1 clove garlic, minced
- 3 tablespoons of Japanese salt-reduced light soy sauce
- 2 tablespoons of mirin
- 1 tablespoon of cooking rice wine
- 3 teaspoons of white vinegar
- ½ tablespoon of rock sugar, roughly pounded
- 1 cup of water
- 400 gm radish, peeled and roughly chopped
- Pinch of salt, to taste
- Spring onion, for garnish

Thickening:

- 2 teaspoons of corn flour / corn starch
- 1 tablespoon of water

Cooking Instructions:

1. Generously season the pork ribs on both sides and set aside. Press the Sauté function and add the pork ribs.

2. Sauté the pork ribs on all sides in two batches. Add all the pork ribs back into the bottom of your Instant Pot. Add in ginger, garlic, soy sauce, mirin, wine, vinegar, rock sugar and water.

3. Close and lock the lid in place and ensure that the valve is in sealing position. Select the "Meat/Stew" function to cook for 35 minutes.

4. When the timer beeps, do a quick pressure release. Carefully open the lid and add in the radish. Close and lock the lid in place.

5. Select the "Meat/Stew" function to cook for 10 minutes. When the timer beeps, do a quick pressure release. Carefully open the lid.

6. Select the Sauté function. Simmer the sauce to reduce by 1/3. Adjust the seasoning with salt.

7. Stir in the thickening and cook until your desired consistency is achieved. Garnish with spring onion.

8. Serve warm and enjoy!

Cuban Shredded Beef Stew

Preparation time: 20 minutes

Cook time: 40 minutes

Total time: 1 hour

Serves: 6-8

- 1 tbsp. of olive oil
- 2 pounds of beef flank steak
- Pinch of salt
- Pepper to taste
- 1 medium onion, sliced
- 4-5 cloves garlic, minced
- 1 cup of beef or chicken broth
- 1 15 ounces can diced tomatoes
- 2 cups of sliced mild/sweet peppers
- ½ tsp. of dried oregano
- 1 tsp. of ground cumin
- 1 bay leaf
- ½ - 1 tsp. of Goya Sazon or Adobo seasoning
- ½ cup of chopped fresh parsley
- 2 tbsp. of vinegar (top choices: white wine, distilled, apple cider)
- ½ cup of chopped green olives

Cooking Instructions:

1. Generously season the flank steak with salt and pepper on each side. Press the Sauté function on your Instant Pot and add the olive oil.

2. Add the meat and cook them to brown on both sides, then transfer them to a bowl. Add the onions and garlic to the pot.

3. Cook, stirring frequently, until the onions start to soften. Add the broth and scrape any browned bits from the bottom of the pot.

4. Add the canned tomatoes, sliced peppers, oregano, cumin, and bay leaf (and seasoning blend, if desired) and give everything a good stir to combine, nestling the browned flank steak into the stew.

5. Close and lock the lid in place and ensure that the valve is in sealing position. Select Manual, High Pressure for 40 minutes.

6. When the timer beeps, do a natural pressure release for about 10 minutes. Carefully open the lid and shred the meat with two forks.

7. Remove the bay leaf, then mix in the parsley, vinegar and green olives. Adjust the seasoning with salt and pepper.

8. Serve with rice and enjoy!

Pork and Pineapple Stew

Serves: 6

Preparation time: 10 minutes

Cook time: 35 minutes

Total time: 45 minutes

Ingredients:

- 1 - 2 tablespoon of bacon fat
- 2 pounds (1kg) stewing pork, cut into 1 inch (2.5 cm) cubes
- 1 tablespoon of coconut amino
- ½ teaspoon of sea salt
- ¼ cup of cassava flour, optional
- ½ teaspoon of ground cloves
- ½ teaspoon of ginger powder
- ½ teaspoon of turmeric powder
- 1 large onion, sliced into wedges
- 2 large cloves garlic, chopped
- 1 teaspoon of ground cinnamon (or a 3 inch cinnamon stick)
- 1 cup bite-sized pineapple chunks (equivalent to ¼ pineapple)
- 1 bay leaf
- 2 tablespoons of kumquat jam
- 1 cup of bone broth
- 1 bunch Swiss chard, stems separated from leaves (stems finely chopped, leaves halved lengthwise and cut into 1 inch thick strips)

Cooking Instructions:

1. First, marinate your pork cubes with the coconut amino, sea salt, cassava flour, ground cloves, ginger powder and turmeric powder for at least 1 hour.

2. Press the Sauté function on your Instant Pot and add the fat. Add the onions and cook for 1 minute.

3. Add the garlic, and sauté until the onions are translucent and the garlic is fragrant. Drain the onions and garlic and set aside.

4. Add more tablespoon of fat/ oil if desired and sauté the marinated pork cubes in batches. Transfer the pork cubes to a bowl and deglaze the pot with the bone broth.

5. Add the pork, onions and garlic back into the bottom of your Instant Pot. Add in the cinnamon, pineapple chunks, finely chopped Swiss chard stems, bay leaf and kumquat jam.

6. Close and lock the lid in place and ensure that the valve is in sealing position. Select the 'Meat/ Stew' function to cook for 35 minutes.

7. When the timer beeps, do a quick pressure release. Carefully open the lid and add in the Swiss chard leaves. Press the Sauté function.

8. Mix together 1 teaspoon of arrowroot starch and 2 teaspoons of water. Add the mixture into the pot and stir.

9. Simmer until the leaves are cooked and the gravy is thickened.

10. Serve and enjoy!

Hoisin Meatballs

Preparation time: 20 minutes

Cook time: 10 minutes

Total time: 30 minutes

Serves: 2 dozen

Ingredients:

- 1 cup of dry red wine or beef broth
- 3 tbsp. of hoisin sauce
- 2 tbsp. of soy sauce
- 1 large egg, lightly beaten
- 4 green onions, chopped
- ¼ cup of finely chopped onion
- ¼ cup of minced fresh cilantro
- 2 garlic cloves, minced
- ½ tsp. of salt
- ½ tsp. of pepper
- 1 lb. of ground beef
- 1 lb. of ground pork
- Sesame seeds

Cooking Instructions:

1. In a medium bowl, whisk together the wine, hoisin sauce and soy sauce. Pour the mixture into the bottom of your Instant Pot.

2. Press the Sauté function and simmer until liquid is reduced slightly. In a separate bowl, combine together the next seven ingredients.

3. Add the beef and pork. Form the mixture into 1-1/2-in. meatballs and add them into the pot. Close and lock the lid in place.

4. Select Manual, High Pressure for 10 minutes. When the timer beeps, do a quick pressure release. Carefully open the lid and sprinkle with sesame seeds.

5. Partially thaw in refrigerator overnight. Microwave, covered, on high for about 8 minutes, stirring through or until heated halfway through.

6. Serve and enjoy!

Beef Curry

Preparation time: 15 minutes

Cook time: 30 minutes

Total time: 45 minutes

Servings: 5

Ingredients:

- 1 pound of grass-fed beef stew meat in chunks
- 2 tablespoons of ghee or coconut oil
- 1 onion, sliced
- 3 large potatoes or sweet potatoes, cut into large chunks
- 6 carrots, cut into large chunks
- 5 cloves garlic, diced
- 1 cup of coconut milk
- ½ cup of bone broth or vegetable broth
- 1 ½ tablespoon of curry powder
- 1 teaspoon of sea salt
- ½ teaspoon of black pepper
- 1 teaspoon of dried oregano
- ¼ teaspoon of paprika

Cooking Instructions:

1. Press the Sauté function on your Instant Pot and add the ghee. Add the onions and garlic and cook for about 2 minutes.

2. Add stew meat and cook on both sides to brown for about 5 minutes. Press the Cancel function.

3. Add the rest of the ingredients including the carrots, potatoes, coconut milk, broth, herbs and spices. Give everything a good stir.

4. Close and lock the lid in place and ensure that the valve is in sealing position. Select the "Meat/Stew" function to cook for 30 minutes.

5. When the timer beeps, do a natural pressure release for about 10 minutes. Carefully remove the lid and stir.

6. Serve over cauliflower rice or white rice and enjoy!

Pork Vindaloo

Servings: 6

Preparation time: 10 minutes

Cook time: 25 minutes Total

time: 35 minutes

Ingredients:

- 3 lb. (1.44 kg) boneless pork shoulder, cubed
- 1 tsp. of sea salt
- ¼ cup (60 ml) olive oil
- 1 large white onion, peeled and finely chopped
- 4 cloves garlic, minced
- 1 piece of fresh ginger, peeled and grated
- 2 tbsp. of vindaloo seasoning or Madras curry
- 1 tsp. of hot paprika
- ½ tsp. of ground turmeric
- 3 tbsp. of all-purpose flour
- 1/3 cup (80 ml) Champagne vinegar
- 1 (14 ½ oz.) can diced tomatoes in juice, undrained
- 1 cup (250 ml) reduced-sodium chicken broth

Cooking Instructions:

1. Sprinkle cubed pork with a slat. Press the Sauté function on your Instant Pot and add the 2 tbsp. of olive oil.

2. Working in batches, sauté the meat in a single layer on both sides, for about 5 to 7 minutes per batch. Remove the browned pork to a bowl.

3. Add the chopped white onion and sauté, stirring frequently for about 3 minutes ot until soft. Stir in garlic, ginger, and spices.

4. Sauté, stirring frequently for additional 30 seconds. Sprinkle in all-purpose flour and give everything a good stir.

5. Add the browned pork back into the Instant Pot. Stir in vinegar, tomatoes with their juice and chicken broth.

6. Deglaze the pot and scrape off any browned bits stuck to the bottom of the pot.

7. Close and lock the lid in place and ensure that the valve is in sealing position. Select Manual, High Pressure for 25 minutes.

8. When the timer beeps, do a quick pressure release. Carefully open the lid and drain the fat from the top of sauce. Sprinkle with fresh chopped cilantro.

9. Serve and enjoy!

Beef Chili

Preparation time: 10 minutes

Cook time: 10 minutes

Total time: 20 minutes

Ingredients:

- 1 pound of ground beef, venison, or turkey
- 2 onions, chopped
- 1 clove garlic, minced
- 1 green peppers
- 28 ounces of diced tomatoes
- 28 ounces of water
- ½ pound of dry kidney beans (soaked overnight) OR 2 (14.5 ounces) cans
- 1 tablespoon of salt
- ½ tablespoon of chili powder
- Dash cayenne pepper

Cooking Instructions:

1. Spray the bottom of your Instant Pot with non-stick cooking. Press the Meat button and brown the meat.

2. Add in the onion and cook for about 7 minutes or until translucent. Press the Cancel function. Add in the rest of the ingredients.

3. Close and lock the lid in place and ensure that the valve is in sealing position. Select the Soup function to cook for 10 minutes.

4. When the timer beeps, do a natural pressure release for about 10 minutes. Carefully remove the lid.

5. Serve and enjoy!

Easy Pork Posole

Preparation time: 30 minutes

Cook time: 10 minutes

Total time: 40 minutes

Yield: 8

Ingredients:

- 1 tbsp. of canola oil
- ½ lb. of boneless pork shoulder butt roast, cubed
- ½ lb. of fully cooked andouille sausage links, sliced
- 2 medium tomatoes, seeded and chopped
- 1 can (15 oz.) hominy, rinsed and drained
- 1 cup of minced fresh cilantro
- 1 onion, chopped
- 4 green onions, chopped
- 1 jalapeno pepper, seeded and chopped
- 2 garlic cloves, minced
- 1 tbsp. of chili powder
- 1 tsp. of ground cumin
- ½ tsp. of cayenne pepper
- ½ tsp. of coarsely ground pepper
- 6 cups reduced-sodium chicken broth
- Corn tortillas, chopped onion, minced fresh cilantro and lime wedges, optional for serving

Cooking Instructions:

1. Press the Sauté function on your Instant Pot and add the oil. Add the pork cubes and sausage.

2. Sauté, stirring frequently until browned. Transfer the pork and sausage; drain. Add the meat back into the pot. Add the remaining ingredients.

3. Close and lock the lid in place and ensure that the valve is in sealing position. Select Manual, High Pressure for 10 minutes.

4. When the timer beeps, do a natural pressure release for about 5 minutes, then quick release any remaining pressure.is closed.

5. Carefully remove the lid and stir. Serve with tortillas, onion, cilantro and lime wedges if desired.

Mesquite Ribs

Preparation time: 10 minutes

Cook time: 35 minutes

Total time: 45 minutes

Serves: 8

Ingredients:

- 1 cup of water
- 2 tbsp. of cider vinegar
- 1 tbsp. of soy sauce
- 4 lb. of pork baby back ribs, cut into serving-size portions
- 2 tbsp. of mesquite seasoning
- ¾ cup of barbecue sauce, divided

Cooking Instructions:

1. Add the water, vinegar and soy sauce into the bottom of your Instant Pot. Season the ribs with mesquite seasoning.

2. Add the ribs into the pot. Close and lock the lid in place and ensure that the valve is in sealing position. Select Manual, High Pressure for 35 minutes.

3. When the timer beeps, do a natural pressure release for about 10 minutes, then quick-release any remaining pressure.

4. Carefully open the lid and transfer the ribs to a foil-lined baking sheet. Brush ribs with barbecue sauce.

5. Add in your broiler and broil for a couple of minutes until glazed. Serve with additional barbecue sauce if desired and enjoy!

Pork Chops with Gravy

Preparation time: 5 minutes

Cook time: 20 minutes

Total time: 25 minutes

Servings: 4

Ingredients:

- 5 pork chops bone in or out
- 1 tbsp. of olive oil
- 1 tsp. of salt
- ½ tsp. of garlic powder
- ½ tsp. of pepper
- 1 envelope ranch dressing mix
- 1 1 oz. of envelope brown gravy mix
- 1 10.5 oz. can cream of chicken soup
- 2 cups of beef broth
- 2 tbsp. of cornstarch
- 2 tbsp. of water

Cooking Instructions:

1. Generously season the pork chops with the salt, garlic powder, and pepper on each side.

2. Press the Sauté function on your Instant Pot and add the olive oil. Add the pork chops and brown per side for 2-3 minutes or until browned.

3. Transfer the pork chops to a bowl. Pour ¼ cup of the beef broth into the bottom of your Instant Pot.

4. Deglaze the pot and scrape off any browned bits stuck to the pot. Press the Cancel function and add the pork chops.

5. Add the ranch dressing mix, brown gravy mix, cream of chicken soup, and remaining beef broth into the Instant Pot.

6. Close and lock the lid in place and ensure that the valve is in sealing position. Select Manual, High Pressure for 8 minutes.

7. When the timer beeps, do a natural pressure release for about 10 minutes, then quick release any remaining pressure.

8. Carefully open the lid and transfer the pork chops to a serving bowl. In a medium bowl, whisk together the cornstarch and water.

9. Press the Sauté function and whisk in the cornstarch mixture. Whisk the content until gravy is thick, then, press the Cancel function.

10. Serve with the gravy and enjoy!

INSTANT POT FISH & SEAFOOD RECIPES

Steamed Alaskan Crab Legs

Preparation time: 10 minutes

Cook time: 4 minutes

Total time: 14 minutes

Ingredients:

- 2-3 lb. of frozen crab legs
- 1 cup of water
- ½ tbsp. of salt
- Butter, melted for serving

Cooking Instructions:

1. Add the steamer basket into the bottom of your Instant Pot and pour 1 cup of water and salt. Add half of the Alaskan King Crab Legs.

2. Close and lock the lid in place and ensure that the valve is in sealing position. Select Manual, High Pressure for 4 minutes.

3. When the timer beeps, do a quick pressure release. Carefully open the lid remove the crab legs. Repeat process with rest of the crab legs.

4. Serve with butter and enjoy!

Lemon Pepper Salmon

Preparation time: 5 minutes

Cook time: 10 minutes

Total time: 15 minutes

Servings: 3 -4

Ingredients:

- ¾ cup of water
- A few sprigs of parsley dill, tarragon, basil or a combo
- 1 lb. of salmon filet skin on
- 3 tsp. of ghee
- ¼ tsp. of salt
- ½ tsp. of pepper
- ½ lemon, thinly sliced
- 1 zucchini, julienned
- 1 red bell pepper, julienned
- 1 carrot, julienned

Cooking Instructions:

1. Add the water and herbs into the bottom of your Instant Pot and place the steamer rack. Add the salmon, skin down on rack.

2. Sprinkle the salmon with ghee, season with salt and pepper, and cover with lemon slices. Close and lock the lid in place and ensure that the valve is in sealing position.

3. Select the "Steam" function to cook for 3 minutes. While salmon cooks, julienne your veggies. When the timer beeps, do a quick pressure release.

4. Press the Cancel function. Carefully open the lid and remove rack with salmon and place on a bowl. Discard the herbs.

5. Add the veggies. Close and lock the lid in place. Select the Sauté function and allow the veggies to cook for about 2 minutes.

6. Add the rest teaspoon of fat into the Instant Pot and pour a little of the sauce over them if desired.

7. Serve with salmon and enjoy!

Bang Bang Shrimp Pasta

Preparation time: 5 minutes

Cook time: 6 minutes

Total time: 11 minutes

Servings: 6

Ingredients:

- 1 lb. of dried spaghetti
- 3 cloves garlic, minced
- 1 tsp. of coconut oil
- 4 ¼ cup of water
- 1 lb. of raw jumbo shrimp, peeled and deveined
- ¾ cup of light mayonnaise
- ¾ cup of Thai sweet chili sauce
- ¼ cup of lime juice
- 1 tbsp. of Sriracha sauce
- ½ cup of chopped scallions
- Pinch of salt
- Pepper to taste

Cooking Instructions:

1. Break up the spaghetti noodles in half and add them into the bottom of your Instant Pot. Place the garlic, coconut oil, 1 tsp. of salt, and water.

2. Close and lock the lid in place and ensure that the valve is in sealing position. Select Manual, High Pressure for 4 minutes.

3. When the timer beeps, do a quick pressure release. Carefully open the lid. In a medium bowl, mix together the mayonnaise, Thai sweet chili sauce, lime juice, and Sriracha.

4. Add the sauce into the pasta. Pour in the shrimp and scallions, and give everything a good stir to combine. Press the Sauté function and cook for 2-3 minutes.

5. Bring the pot to a boil and simmer until the shrimp are pink. Season with salt and pepper to taste. Add more Sriracha if desired.

6. Serve hot and enjoy!

Sweet and Spicy Pineapple Shrimp

Preparation time: 10 minutes

Cook time: 2 minutes

Total time: 12 minutes

Servings: 4

Ingredients:

- 1 large red bell pepper, sliced
- 12 oz. of Calrose rice or quinoa
- ¾ cup of unsweetened pineapple juice
- ¼ cup of dry white wine
- ¼ cup of fresh water
- 2 tbsp. of soy sauce
- 2 tbsp. of Thai sweet chili sauce
- 1 tbsp. of sambal Oelek ground chili paste
- 1 lb. of large shrimp frozen w/ tails
- 4 Scallions chopped, white and greens separated
- 1.5 cups of pineapple chunks drained

Cooking Instructions:

1. Drain the pineapple juice and reserve the pineapple chunks aside. Measure out ¾ cup of pineapple juice.

2. Add the red bell peppers, pineapple juice, wine, water, chili sauce, soy sauce, sambal Oelek, rice and chopped scallions into the bottom of your Instant Pot.

3. Add the frozen Shrimp on top. Close and lock the lid in place and ensure that the valve is in sealing position.

4. Select Manual, High Pressure for 2 minutes. When the timer beeps, do a natural pressure release for about 10 minutes.

5. Carefully remove the lid and add the pineapple chunks and scallion greens and give everything a good.

6. Serve and enjoy!

Shrimp Paella

Preparation time: 10 minutes

Cook time: 5 minutes

Total time: 15 minutes

Servings: 4

Ingredients:

- 1 pound of jumbo shrimp, shell and tail on frozen
- 1 cup of Jasmine rice
- 4 tablespoons of butter
- 1 onion, chopped
- 4 cloves garlic, chopped
- 1 red pepper, chopped
- 1 cup of chicken broth
- ½ cup of white wine
- 1 teaspoon of paprika
- 1 teaspoon of turmeric
- ½ teaspoon of salt
- ¼ teaspoon of black pepper
- 1 pinch saffron threads
- ¼ teaspoon of red pepper flakes
- ¼ cup of cilantro, optional

Cooking Instructions:

1. Press the Sauté function on your Instant Pot and add the butter. Add the onions and sauté until softened.

2. Add the garlic and sauté for about 1 minute. Add the paprika, turmeric, salt, black pepper, red pepper flakes, and saffron threads and cook for 1 more minute.

3. Add the red peppers, rice and give everything a good stir. Cook for additional 1 minute. Add the chicken broth and white wine.

4. Add the shrimp on top. Close and lock the lid in place and ensure that the valve is in sealing position. Select Manual, High Pressure for 5 minutes.

5. When the timer beeps, do a quick pressure release. Carefully open the lid and transfer the shrimp to a bowl and peel if desired.

6. Serve with cilantro and enjoy!

Fish Tacos

Preparation time: 10 minutes

Cook time: 8 minutes

Total time: 18 minutes

Ingredients:

- 2 tilapia fillets
- 1 tsp. of canola oil
- Pinch of salt
- 2 tbsp. of smoked paprika
- Juice of 1 lime
- 1-2 sprigs of fresh or dry cilantro

Cooking Instructions:

1. Add the tilapia fillets in the center of a large piece of parchment paper. Drizzle with the canola oil, sprinkle with salt and paprika.

2. Squeeze the lime juice on the tilapia and sprinkle with some cilantro. Gently fold the parchment paper into a packet.

3. Pour 1 ½ cups of water into the inner liner of your Instant Pot and place the trivet. Add the parchment packet on top of the trivet.

4. Close and lock the lid in place and ensure that the valve is in sealing position. Select Manual, High Pressure for 8 minutes.

5. When the timer beeps, do a quick pressure release. Carefully open the lid and cut the fish as you desire to add on a taco. Build your taco your way.

6. Serve and enjoy!

Drunken Clams

Servings: 4-6

Preparation time: 10 minutes

Cook time: 4 minutes

Total time: 14 minutes

Ingredients:

- ¼ cup of olive oil
- 2 cloves garlic, peeled and minced
- ¼ cup of finely chopped fresh basil
- 2 cups of pale ale
- 1 cup of water
- ½ cup of chicken broth
- ¼ cup of dry white wine
- 3 lb. of fresh clams, scrabbled
- 2 tbsp. of freshly squeezed lemon juice

Cooking Instructions:

1. Press the Sauté function on your Instant Pot and add the minced garlic. Sauté for about 2 minutes, or until fragrant.

2. Stir in chopped fresh basil. Add water, beer, chicken broth, wine and lemon juice. Cook for about 1 minute to bring the mixture to a boil.

3. Place the trivet and steamer basket into the bottom of your Instant Pot. Add the clams in basket. Close and lock the lid in place.

4. Select Manual, High Pressure for 4 minutes. When the timer beeps, do a quick pressure release.

5. Carefully remove the lid and discard any clams that have not opened.

6. Place the cooked clams to a serving plate. Pour the cooking liquid over.

7. Serve immediately and enjoy!

Seafood Gumbo

Servings: 8

Preparation time: 10 minutes

Cook time: 5 minutes

Total time: 15 minutes

Ingredients:

- 24 oz. of sea bass filets patted dry and cut into 2" chunks
- 3 tbsp. of ghee or avocado oil
- 3 tbsp. of Cajun seasoning or creole seasoning
- 2 yellow onions, diced
- 2 bell peppers, diced
- 4 celery ribs, diced
- 28 oz. of diced tomatoes
- ¼ cup of tomato paste
- 3 bay leaves
- 1 ½ cups of bone broth
- 2 lb. of medium to large raw shrimp deveined
- Pinch of sea salt
- Black pepper to taste

Cooking Instructions:

1. Generously season the barramundi with some salt and pepper to coat. Sprinkle the fish with half of the Cajun seasoning and set aside.

2. Add the ghee into the bottom of your Instant Pot. Press the "Sauté" function and add the barramundi chunks. Cook them on both sides for about 4 minutes.

3. Place the fish to a large bowl with a slotted spoon. Add the onions, pepper, celery and the remaining Cajun seasoning to the Instant Pot.

4. Cook for about 2 minutes or until fragrant. Press the Cancel function and add the cooked fish. Add the diced tomatoes, tomato paste, bay leaves and bone broth.

5. Give everything a good stir. Close and lock the lid in place and ensure that the valve is in sealing position. Select Manual, High Pressure for 5 minutes.

6. When the timer beeps, do a quick pressure release. Carefully open the lid and add the shrimp.

7. Press the Sauté function and cook for about 4 minutes, or until the shrimp have turned opaque.

8. Season with more sea salt and black pepper, to taste. Serve warm and top with some cauliflower rice and chives.

9. Serve immediately and enjoy!

Chipotle Shrimp Soup

Preparation time: 5 minutes

Cook time: 25 minutes

Total time: 30 minutes

Servings: 5

Ingredients:

- 3 slices bacon, chopped
- 1 cup of onion diced
- ¾ cup of celery chopped
- 1 teaspoon of garlic
- 1 tablespoon of flour
- ¼ cup of dry white wine
- 1 ½ cups of chicken or vegetable broth
- ½ cup of whole milk
- 1 ½ cups of potatoes, cut into small (1/3-inch) cubes
- 1 cup of frozen corn kernels
- 2 teaspoon of diced canned chipotle peppers in adobo sauce
- ¾ teaspoon of salt
- ½ teaspoon of ground black pepper
- ½ teaspoon of dried thyme
- ½ pound of shrimp, peeled and deveined
- ¼ cup of heavy cream

Cooking Instructions:

1. Press the Sauté button on your Instant Pot and add the bacon. Cook the bacon, stirring frequently until crisp, for about 3 minutes.

2. Add the onions, celery and garlic. Cook for about 3 minutes or until the vegetables have softened. Stir in flour and sauté for additional 1 minute.

3. Press the Cancel button and deglaze the pot with white wine to scrape off any browned bits stuck to the bottom of the pot.

4. Add in broth, milk, potatoes, corn, chipotle, salt, black pepper and thyme. Close and lock the lid in place and ensure that the valve is in sealing position.

5. Select Manual, High Pressure for 1 minute. When the timer beeps, do a quick pressure release. Carefully open the lid and stir in shrimp and cream.

6. Close and lock the lid in place. Let the shrimp cook in the residual heat for about 10 minutes. Garnish with scallions, parsley and/or crumbled bacon.

7. Serve and enjoy!

Shrimp Scampi Paella

Servings: 4

Preparation time: 10 minutes

Cook time: 5 minutes

Total time: 15 minutes

Ingredients:

- 1 lb. of frozen wild caught shrimp, 16-20 count shell & tail on
- 1 cup of Jasmine rice
- ¼ cup of organic Grass-Fed butter or ghee
- ¼ cup of fresh parsley, chopped
- 1 tsp. of sea salt
- ¼ tsp. of black pepper
- 1 pinch of crushed red pepper flakes or to taste
- 1 medium lemon, juiced
- 1 pinch saffron
- 1 ½ cups of water, filtered or chicken broth
- 4 cloves garlic, minced
- Optional garnishes: organic Grass-Fed butter or ghee, grated hard cheese, parmesan, romano or asiago, fresh parsley, chopped, lemon, juiced

Cooking Instructions:

1. Add all of the ingredients into the bottom of your Instant Pot, placing the frozen shell on shrimp on top.

2. Close and lock the lid in place and ensure that the valve is in sealing position. Select Manual, High Pressure for 5 minutes.

3. When the timer beeps, do a quick pressure release. Carefully open the lid. Remove the cooked shrimp and peel.

4. Place the peeled shrimp back into the rice and discard the shells. Serve with a garnish of fresh parsley, butter, grated cheese and squeeze of lemon juice.

5. Serve and enjoy!

INSTANT POT EGG RECIPES

Breakfast Egg Casserole

Preparation time: 8

Preparation time: 10 minutes

Cook time: 12 minutes

Total time: 22 minutes

Ingredients:

- 3 slices of bacon, chopped
- 1 pound of turkey breakfast sausage
- 1/4 teaspoon salt
- ¼ cup of chopped onion
- 10 large eggs
- 2/3 cup of milk
- ¼ tsp. of salt
- 2 cloves minced garlic
- ½ tsp. of dried basil
- ½ tsp. of dried oregano
- 1 ½ cup. of shredded Italian blend cheese
- 1 cup of water
- 2 ounces of crumbled feta

Cooking Instructions:

1. Press the Sauté function on your Instant Pot and add the chopped bacon. Sauté the chopped bacon until browned and set aside.

2. Add the sausage to the pot and sauté until no longer pink. Add the onions and cook for about 4 minutes or until onions have softened. Transfer the sausage to a bowl and set aside.

3. Add all but 1 tbsp. of chopped bacon to the sausage mixture. Spray an 8-inch spring form pan with non-stick spray and place a piece of foil at the bottom.

4. In a medium bowl, whisk together the eggs, milk, salt, garlic, basil, and oregano. Arrange the cheese on the bottom of the pan, and place the meat mixture.

5. Pour egg mixture over the meat. Pour 1 cup of water into the bottom of your Instant Pot and place the trivet. Add the baking pan on top of the trivet.

6. Close and lock the lid in place and ensure that the valve is in sealing position. Select Manual, High Pressure for 12 minutes.

7. When the timer beeps, do a quick pressure release. Carefully open the lid and let the casserole to rest for about 10 minutes.

8. Top with feta cheese and the rest of the bacon.

9. Serve immediately and enjoy!

Eggs in Marinara Sauce

Preparation time: 5 minutes

Cook time: 11 minutes

Total time: 17 minutes

Ingredients:

- 1 tablespoon of coconut oil
- 2 garlic cloves, minced
- ½ onion, diced
- 1 red bell pepper, diced
- 1 teaspoon of chili powder
- ½ teaspoon of paprika
- ½ teaspoon of ground cumin
- Pinch of salt
- Pepper, to taste
- 1 ½ cup of sugar-free marinara sauce
- 4-6 eggs
- Chopped fresh parsley leaves, for garnish

Cooking Instructions:

1. Press the Sauté function on your Instant Pot and add the coconut oil. Add the garlic, onion, red bell pepper, chili powder, and paprika cumin.

2. Generously season with salt and pepper. Sauté, stirring for about 5 minutes, or until the onion is translucent. Add the marinara sauce and give everything a good stir.

3. Press the Cancel function and allow to rest for about 5 minutes. Crack the eggs into the sauce, and ensure that the yolks are not cracked.

4. Close and lock the lid in place and ensure that the valve is in sealing position. Select Manual, Low Pressure for 0 minute. When the timer beeps, do a quick pressure release.

5. Carefully remove the lid and sprinkle with parsley leaves. Serve and enjoy!

Perfect Poached Egg

Preparation time: 3 minutes

Cook time: 6-8 minutes

Total time: about 15 minutes

Serves: 1-7 eggs

Ingredients:

- Eggs (from 1-7 eggs)
- Pinch of salt
- Pepper, to taste

Cooking Instructions:

1. Pour 1 cup of water into the bottom of your Instant Pot and place the trivet inside. Spray the silicone tray with nonstick cooking spray.

2. Crack the number of eggs your need into the holes of the silicone tray. Add the tray on top of the trivet.

3. Close and lock the lid in place and ensure that the valve is in sealing position. Select Manual, High Pressure for 6 to 8 minutes.

4. When the timer beeps, do a quick pressure release. Carefully open the lid and check the eggs. They should appear white and yellow middle will be slightly jiggly.

5. Carefully scrape the edges with a soft edge knife or spoon to loosen and scoop it from the tray. Sprinkle with salt and pepper.

6. Serve immediately on avocado toast, muffins, tamales, salads, hash browns, if desired and enjoy!

Crustless Quiche

Preparation time: 10 minutes

Cook time: 30 minutes

Total time: 40 minutes

Servings: 4

Ingredients:

- 6 large eggs, well beaten
- ½ cup of milk
- ¼ tsp. of salt
- 1/8 tsp. of ground black pepper
- 4 slices bacon, cooked and crumbled
- 1 cup of cooked ground sausage
- ½ cup of diced ham
- 2 large green onions, chopped
- 1 cup of shredded cheese

Cooking Instructions:

1. Pour 1 cup of water into the bottom of your Instant Pot and place the trivet inside. In a medium bowl, whisk together the eggs, milk, salt, and pepper.

2. Add the bacon, sausage, ham, green onions, and cheese to a 1 ½ quart soufflé dish and give everything a good mix.

3. Add the egg mixture over the top of the meat and give everything a good stir to combine. Loosely cover the soufflé dish with a piece of aluminum foil.

4. Place the dish on the trivet in the Instant Pot. Close and lock the lid in place and ensure that the valve is in sealing position.

5. Select Manual, High Pressure for 30 minutes. When the timer beeps, do a quick pressure release. Carefully remove the lid and take out the soufflé dish.

6. Remove the aluminum foil and sprinkle the top of the quiche with more cheese and broil until melted and lightly browned.

7. Serve and enjoy!

Ham and Egg Casserole

Preparation time: 10 minutes

Cook time: 25 minutes

Total time: 35 minutes

Ingredients:

- 4 small red potatoes
- ½ onion, diced
- 1 cup of chopped ham
- 2 cups of shredded cheddar cheese
- 10 large eggs ◻ 1 cup of milk
- 1 tsp. of salt
- 1 tsp. of pepper

Cooking Instructions:

1. Spray your Instant Pot insert with nonstick cooking spray. Place the eggs and milk into the bowl and give everything a good whisk until well blended.

2. Add the potatoes, ham, onions, cheese, and salt and pepper in with the eggs and give everything a good mix until to coat with the egg mixture.

3. Lightly cover the bowl with foil. Pour 2 cups of water into the bottom of your Instant Pot and place the steam rack.

4. Place the bowl covered with foil on top of the steam rack. Close and lock the lid in place and ensure that the valve is in sealing position.

5. Select Manual, High Pressure for 25 minutes. When the timer beeps, do a quick pressure release. Carefully open the lid.

6. Serve with your desired toppings like: sour cream, salsa, avocado, more cheese tomatoes, and salt and pepper!

Cheesy Egg Bake

Preparation time: 5 minutes

Cook time: 20 minutes

Total time: 25 minutes

Serves: 4

Ingredients:

- 6 slices bacon, chopped into small pieces
- 2 cups of frozen hash browns
- 6 large eggs
- ¼ cup of milk
- ½ cup of shredded cheddar cheese
- 1 tsp. of kosher salt
- ½ tsp. of pepper
- Optional: onion, red pepper, spinach, mushrooms, green onions

Cooking Instructions:

1. Press the Sauté function on your Instant Pot and add the chopped bacon. Cook the bacon until crispy.

2. Add in any extra veggies that you desired and cook them for about 3 minutes or until tender. Add in frozen hash browns and give everything a good stir until slightly thawed, about 2 minutes.

3. Grease a heat proof container that will fit into your Instant Pot with nonstick cooking oil. In a medium bowl, whisk together the eggs, milk, shredded cheese, and salt and pepper.

4. Add the bacon and veggie mixture to the eggs. Pour the egg mixture into your greased, heat proof container. Add 1 ½ cups of water into the bottom of your Instant Pot and place the trivet inside.

5. Add the heat proof bowl with egg mixture on top of trivet. Close and lock the lid in place and ensure that the valve is in sealing position.

6. Select Manual, High Pressure for 20 minutes. When the timer beeps, do a quick pressure release. Carefully open the lid and loosen edges with knife and flip onto large bowl.

7. Serve with green onions and extra shredded cheese!

Mexican Egg Casserole

Preparation time: 10 minutes

Cook time: 25 minutes

Total time: 35 minutes

Serves: 8

Ingredients:

- 8 large eggs, beaten
- 1 lb. of mild ground sausage
- ½ red onion, chopped
- 1 red bell pepper, chopped
- 1 can black beans, rinsed
- ½ cup of green onions
- ½ cup of flour
- 1 cup of Cotija cheese
- 1 cup of mozzarella cheese
- Optional: Sour cream, cilantro

Cooking Instructions:

1. Press the Sauté function on your Instant Pot and add the sausage and onion. Sauté for about 6 minutes or until the sausage is cooked through.

2. In a medium bowl, mix together the flour with eggs until combined. Add the egg mixture to Instant Pot. Add the chopped vegetables, beans and cheeses.

3. Set some mozzarella cheese aside to place on top of the casserole. Close and lock the lid in place and ensure that the valve is in sealing position.

4. Select Manual, High Pressure for 20 minutes. When the timer beeps, do a quick pressure release. Carefully open the lid and remove the casserole.

5. Loosen the edges with a knife and flip it upside down onto a serving bowl. Add the rest of the cheese on top of the casserole.

6. Allow it to rest for a few minutes until the cheese melted.

7. Serve and enjoy!

Hard Boiled Eggs

Preparation time: 10 minutes

Cook time: 5 minutes

Total time: 15 minutes

Servings: 12

Ingredients:

- 12 large eggs
- 1 cup of water

Cooking Instructions:

1. Pour 1 cup of water into the bottom of your Instant Pot and place the steam rack inside. Add your desired number of eggs on the rack.

2. Close and lock the lid in place and ensure that the valve is in sealing position. Select Manual, High Pressure for 5 minutes.

3. When the timer beeps, do a quick pressure release. Carefully open the lid and remove the eggs. Place the eggs in ice water bath.

4. Allow the eggs to rest for about 5 minutes. Remove eggs from water bath and peel the shell. Refrigerate for at least 7 days.

5. Serve and enjoy!

Mini Frittatas

Preparation time: 10 minutes

Cook time: 10 minutes

Total time: 20 minutes

Servings: 3

Ingredients:

- 4 slices turkey bacon chopped, uncooked
- 6 large eggs
- 1 tsp. of salt
- 1 tsp. of pepper
- 1 medium red potato, diced
- ½ bell pepper, diced
- ½ medium onion, diced
- ¼ cup of milk
- ¼ cup of cheddar cheese

Cooking Instructions:

1. Add the chopped turkey bacon into the bottom of three heat-proof ramekins. Add the diced vegetables on top of the bacon.

2. In a medium bowl, mix together the eggs, milk, salt, and pepper. Pour the eggs mixture over the veggies and sprinkle shredded cheese on top.

3. Lightly cover each ramekin with a piece of aluminum foil. Pour 1 cup of water into the bottom of your Instant Pot and place the trivet. Place the bowl on top the trivet.

4. Close and lock the lid in place and ensure that the valve is in sealing position. Select Manual, High Pressure for 10 minutes.

5. When the timer beeps, do a quick pressure release. Carefully open the lid and remove the heat-proof containers. Loosen the edges with knife and flip onto a serving bowl.

6. Serve and enjoy!

Eggs en Cocotte

Preparation time: 15 minutes

Cook time: 2 minutes

Total time: 17 minutes

Servings: 3

Ingredients:

- Butter, room temp
- 3 tbsp. of cream
- 3 fresh pasture raised eggs
- 1 tbsp. of chives
- Pinch of sea salt
- Freshly ground pepper
- 1 cup of water

Cooking Instructions:

1. Add 1 tbsp. of cream into each ramekin and crack an egg into each ramekin. Sprinkle with chives.

2. Place the rack into the inner liner of your Instant Pot and pour 1 cup of water. Place ramekins on top of the rack.

3. Close and lock the lid in place and ensure that the valve is in sealing position. Select Manual, High Pressure for 2 minutes.

4. When the timer beeps, do a quick pressure release. Carefully open the lid and remove the ramekins from the Instant Pot. Season with sea salt and pepper.

5. Serve on toast and enjoy!

INSTANT POT BEAN & GRAIN RECIPES
Lora's Red Beans & Rice

Preparation time: 15 minutes

Cook time: 30 minutes

Total time: 45 minutes

Serves: 10

Ingredients:

- 1 package (16 oz.) dried kidney beans (about 2 ½ cups)
- 2 cups of cubed fully cooked ham (about 1 lb.)
- 1 package (12 oz.) fully cooked andouille chicken sausage links, sliced
- 1 small green pepper, chopped
- 1 small onion, chopped
- 2 celery ribs, chopped
- 1 tbsp. of hot pepper sauce
- 2 garlic cloves, minced
- 1 tsp. of salt
- Hot cooked rice

Cooking Instructions:

1. Rinse and sort beans. Soak the beans for at least 6 hours according to package directions.

2. Drain and remove the water, rinse with cool water. Add together the ham, sausage, vegetables, pepper sauce, garlic, and salt into the bottom of your Instant Pot.

3. Pour about 4 cups of water to cover the ingredients in the pot. Close and lock the lid in place and ensure that the valve is in sealing position.

4. Select Manual, High Pressure for 30 minutes. When the timer beeps, do a quick pressure release. Carefully open the lid and stir.

5. Serve with rice and enjoy!

Spanish Rice with Beef Sirloin or Flank Steak

Preparation time: 9 minutes

Cook time: 21 minutes

Total time: 30 minutes

Servings: 4

Ingredients:

- 1 tablespoon of extra-virgin olive oil
- 1 lb. of frozen sirloin or flank steak
- ½ medium onion, chopped
- 2 cloves garlic, minced
- 1 teaspoon of chipotle chili powder
- ½ teaspoon of ground cumin
- 1 cup of long-grain white rice, rinsed
- 2 cups of low-sodium beef broth
- 16 ounces red salsa, store-bought or 2 cups homemade salsa
- 15 ounces canned black beans, or 2 cups cooked black beans
- 15 ounces canned fire-roasted corn, drained (We used 1 ¾ cups of frozen)
- 1 ¾ cups of homemade tomato sauce
- Coarse salt and freshly ground black pepper

Cooking Instructions:

1. Press the Sauté function on your Instant Pot and add the olive oil. Add the frozen sirloin and cook for about 4 minutes to brown on both sides. Set the sirloin aside.

2. Add the onion and sauté for 5 minutes, until it's soft. Add the garlic, chili powder and cumin and sauté for additional 1 minute. Press the Cancel function.

3. Add the rice, reserved sirloin and beef broth to the pot, and give everything a good stir to remove any browned bits from the bottom. Add the salsa, black beans, corn and tomatoes.

4. Close and lock the lid in place and ensure that the valve is in sealing position. Select Manual, High Pressure for 10 minutes. When the timer beeps, do a quick pressure release. Carefully open the lid and remove the sirloin.

5. Shred the sirloin with two forks, and return back to the pot. Season with salt and pepper and give everything a good mix to combine.

6. Serve and enjoy!

Mexican Beef Rice

Preparation time: 9 minutes

Cook time: 16 minutes

Total time: 25 minutes

Servings: 4 - 6 servings

Ingredients:

- 1 tbsp. of olive oil
- 1 lb. of lean ground beef ◻ 1 cup of diced red onion
- 1 tsp. of chili powder, Hatch chile powder is okay
- ½ tsp. of ground cumin
- ½ tsp. of salt
- 1 cup of long grain white rice, rinsed well and drained
- 2 cups of water
- 2 cups of chunky salsa
- 15 oz. of black beans rinsed and drained
- 1 cup of cooked corn kernels
- 2 tbsp. of chopped fresh cilantro
- 1 cup of shredded cheese Cheddar, Monterey Jack and Cheddar, or 4 Cheese Mexican blend
- Boston lettuce optional for serving

Cooking Instructions:

1. Press the Sauté function on your Instant Pot and add the ground beef. Add the onion, chili powder, cumin, and salt.

2. Sauté, stirring frequently until beef has browned, about 5 minutes. Add the rice, water, and salsa and give everything a good stir to combine.

3. Close and lock the lid in place and ensure that the valve is in sealing position. Select Manual, High Pressure for 8 minutes.

4. When the timer beeps, do a quick pressure release. Carefully open the lid add the black beans, corn, and cilantro. Stir to combine.

5. Press the Sauté function and cook, stirring occasionally, about 3 minutes. Transfer to a serving bowl. Top with cheese and serve with Boston lettuce leaves to make lettuce wraps, if desired.

Black Bean & Rice Burritos

Preparation time: 10 minutes

Cook time: 10 minutes

Total time: 20 minutes

Ingredients:

- 2 cups of brown long-grained rice or brown rice blend
- 1 cup of pre-soaked black beans
- 1 tablespoon of chili powder
- 1 tablespoon of cumin
- 1 teaspoon of paprika
- 1 medium onion, chopped
- 2 garlic cloves, minced
- Dash of olive oil
- 1 cup of salsa or pureed tomatoes
- 1 teaspoon of better-than-bouillon veggie bouillon
- 2 cups of water

Cooking Instructions:

1. Press the Sauté function on your Instant Pot and add the olive oil. Add the onions and garlic and cook until translucent.

2. Add 2 cups of brown rice blend, and 2 cups of water into the bottom of your Instant Pot. Close and lock the lid in place and ensure that the valve is in sealing position.

3. Select Manual, High Pressure for 12 minutes. When the timer beeps, do a quick pressure release. Carefully open the lid.

4. Add the beans, spices, tomato puree, better-than-bouillon, and remaining 1.5 cups of water into the pot. Close and lock the lid in place.

5. Select Manual, High Pressure for 10 minutes. When the timer beeps, do a natural pressure release for about 15 minutes. Carefully open the lid and season with salt.

6. Serve in a tortilla with fresh scallions, chopped tomatoes, avocado and fresh cilantro and enjoy!

Pinto Beans

Preparation time: 10 minutes

Cook time: 1 hour 5 minutes

Total time: 1 hour 15 minutes

Ingredients:

- 2 strips uncooked bacon
- 1 medium onion, diced
- 4 cups of low-sodium chicken broth
- 1 ½ cups of water
- 1 ¼ teaspoon of garlic powder
- 1 ¼ teaspoon of kosher sea salt
- 1 teaspoon of chili powder
- ½ teaspoon of cumin
- ½ teaspoon of coriander
- ½ teaspoon of paprika
- ¼ teaspoon of ground black pepper
- 1/8 teaspoon of cayenne pepper
- 1 pound of pinto beans, rinsed and picked through

Cooking Instructions:

1. Turn Instant Pot on Sauté function and add the bacon. Sauté the bacon for 2 minutes, turn the bacon to cook on both sides.

2. Add the onion and stir, cook for additional 2 minutes. Pour in the broth and water. Add together the garlic powder, salt, chili powder, cumin, and coriander.

3. Add the paprika, black pepper, cayenne pepper, and pinto beans into the bottom of your Instant Pot. Close and lock the lid in place.

4. Select Manual, High Pressure for 47 minutes. When the timer beeps, do a natural pressure release for about 15 minutes.

5. Carefully open the lid and remove the bacon. Stir and allow it to sit for about 5 minutes before serving. Garnish with cilantro if desired.

6. Serve and enjoy!

Refried Beans

Preparation time: 15 minutes

Cook time: 65 minutes

Total time: 1 hour 20 minutes

Servings: 10

Ingredients:

- 1 lb. of dried pinto beans (2 cups)
- 7 cups of water
- 1 cup of onion, chopped
- 3 cloves garlic, minced
- 1 tsp. of kosher salt
- 1 tsp. of ground cumin
- ½ tsp. of dried leaf oregano
- ½ tsp. of freshly ground black pepper
- 3 tbsp. of bacon drippings (or lard, or olive oil)
- A dash of cayenne pepper, optional

Cooking Instructions:

1. Rinse and sort the pinto beans in a large bowl of water. Add the pinto beans to the Instant Pot. Add the water, onion, garlic, 1 tbsp. of salt, and cumin.

2. Add the oregano, pepper, bacon drippings, lard, or oil, and a dash of cayenne pepper, if desired. Close and lock the lid in place and set valve to the sealing position.

3. Select the Bean/Chili function and adjust to cook for 45 minutes. When the timer beeps, do a natural pressure release for about 15 minutes.

4. Carefully open the lid and drain the beans with a colander or large sieve over a large bowl. Set the liquids aside. Add the beans in a separate bowl and puree them with an immersion blender.

5. Add some of the reserved liquids to achieve your preferred consistency. Season with more salt and ladle into individual bowls. Top with jalapeños, if desired.

6. Serve with a garnish of shredded cheese, chopped red or green onions, chopped cilantro, diced tomatoes, sour cream, salsa, or guacamole.

Mexican Rice with Corn and Bell Peppers

Preparation time: 10 minutes

Cook time: 15 minutes

Total time: 25 minutes

Serves: 4

Ingredients:

- 3 tbsp. of oil
- ¾ cup of finely chopped onions
- 3 garlic cloves, minced
- 2 tsp. of ground chipotle chili powder
- 1 cup of basmati rice (or long grain rice)
- 1 cup of tomato puree
- ¾ cup of corn kernels (fresh or frozen)
- 1 cup of bell peppers, cut into juliennes
- 1 tsp. of roasted cumin powder
- 1 ½ cups of vegetable stock
- 1 ½ tsp. of salt
- Sour cream, for topping
- Chopped coriander leaves, for topping

Cooking Instructions:

1. Press the Sauté function on your Instant Pot and add the oil. Add the onions, and garlic and sauté, stirring for 2 minutes or until the onions are translucent.

2. Add the chipotle powder and rice and give everything a good stir to coat the rice with the oil. Sauté the rice for about 4 minutes, stirring occasionally.

3. Add the sweet corn, tomato puree, stock, cumin powder and salt and give everything a good stir. Close and lock the lid in place.

4. Select Manual, High Pressure for 8 minutes. When the timer beeps, do a quick pressure release. Carefully open the lid and stir in the bell peppers.

5. Close and lock the lid again for 10 minutes to cook the peppers, while keeping them crunchy. Top with chopped coriander and sour cream, if desired.

6. Serve and enjoy!

Hamburger and Rice

Preparation time: 10 minutes

Cook time: 10 minutes

Total time: 20 minutes

Ingredients:

- 1 lb. of ground beef
- ½ onion, diced
- 1 can cream of mushroom soup
- 2 ½ cups of chicken broth
- 1 cup of rice
- 2 tbsp. of olive oil
- 2 stalks celery, diced

Cooking Instructions:

1. Press the Sauté function on your Instant Pot and sauté the hamburger, onion and celery and drain grease.

2. In a medium bowl, combine together the chicken broth and can of cream of mushroom soup until smooth. Pour the mixture over the hamburger mixture.

3. Sprinkle rice on top of the ingredients. Close and lock the lid in place and ensure that the valve is in sealing position.

4. Select Manual, High Pressure for 10 minutes. When the timer beeps, do a quick pressure release.

5. Carefully remove the lid and give everything a good stir. Allow it to rest for about 5 minutes before serving.

6. Serve and enjoy!

INSTANT POT VEGAN & VEGETARIAN RECIPES

Potato Corn Chowder

Preparation time: 25 minutes

Cook time: 5 minutes

Total time: 30 minutes

Servings: 6

Ingredients:

- 1 cup of diced onion
- 2 cloves garlic, minced
- 1 cup of diced carrots
- 1 cup of diced celery
- 6 cups of diced yellow potatoes (about 6 small potatoes)
- 1 bay leaf
- 1 tsp. of dried thyme
- 4 cups of vegetable broth
- 2 cups of frozen corn defrosted
- ½ cup of raw cashews
- ½ cup of water
- Pinch of salt
- Pepper to taste

Cooking Instructions:

1. Turn the Instant Pot on Sauté function and add the onion. Add a splash of water and cook for a few minutes or until the onion has softened.

2. Add the garlic and cook for additional 30 seconds. Add the carrots and celery and cook for a couple of minutes until the vegetables begin to soften.

3. Select the Cancel function and add the potatoes. Add the bay leaf, thyme, and vegetable broth into the bottom of your Instant Pot and give everything a good stir.

4. Close and lock the lid in place and ensure that the valve is in sealing position. Select Manual, High Pressure for 4 minutes.

5. Add together the cashews and water in a high-speed blender to make the cashew cream. Blend everything until completely smooth.

6. When the timer beeps, do a quick pressure release. Carefully open the lid. Add the corn and give everything a good stir.

7. Pour in the cashew cream and give everything a good stir to combine. Season with salt and pepper to taste.

8. Serve and enjoy!

Vegan BBQ Meatballs

Preparation time: 5 minutes

Cook time: 15 minutes

Total time: 20 minutes

Ingredients:

- ¼ cup of water
- 1 ½ - 2 lb. of frozen vegan meatballs (We used 2 bags of Trader Joe's meatballs)
- 1 ½ cups of barbeque sauce
- 1 14 oz. can of whole berry cranberry sauce
- 1 tbsp. of cornstarch mixed with 1 tbsp. of water

Cooking Instructions:

1. Pour the water into the bottom of your Instant Pot and add the frozen meatballs on top. Place the barbeque sauce on top of the meatballs.

2. Mash up the cranberry sauce and add them over the barbeque sauce, and cover the meatballs with a spoon. Close and lock the lid in place.

3. Select Manual, High Pressure for 5 minutes. When the timer beeps, do a natural pressure release for about 10 minutes.

4. Carefully open the lid and add the cornstarch slurry mixture into the pot. Give everything a good stir. Press the Sauté function.

5. Sauté, stirring for about 3 minutes to thicken slightly and bubble. Press the Cancel function. Ladle into individual bowl.

6. Serve and enjoy!

Pasta Puttanesca

Preparation time: 10 minutes

Cook time 5 minutes

Total time 15 minutes

Servings: 4

Ingredients:

- 3 cloves garlic, minced
- 4 cups of pasta sauce (homemade or store-bought)
- 3 cups of water
- 4 cups of pasta such as penne or fusilli
- ¼ tsp. of crushed red pepper flakes
- 1 tbsp. of capers
- ½ cup of Kalamata olives, sliced
- Salt to taste
- Pepper to taste

Cooking Instructions:

1. Turn the Instant Pot on Sauté function and add the garlic.

2. Cook the garlic in a splash of water for about 30 seconds. Press the Cancel function.

3. Add the pasta sauce, water, pasta, crushed red pepper flakes, capers, and olives into the bottom of your Instant Pot and stir.

4. Close and lock the lid the lid in place. Select Manual, High Pressure for 5 minutes. When the timer beeps, do a quick pressure release.

5. Carefully open the lid and stir the pasta. Season with salt and pepper, if desired.

6. Serve and enjoy!

Garlic Hummus

Preparation time: 5 minutes

Cook time: 40 minutes

Total time: 45 minutes

Servings: 12

Ingredients:

- 1 ½ cups of dried chickpeas, rinsed
- 6 cups of water
- ½ cup of tahini
- 2 cloves garlic
- 3 tbsp. of lemon juice, about 2 medium lemons
- 1 ½ tsp. of salt
- ½ - ¾ cup of bean cooking liquid
- Crushed red pepper, chopped parsley, paprika optional

Cooking Instructions:

1. Add the chickpeas along with water into the bottom of your Instant Pot. Close and lock the lid in place and ensure that the valve is in sealing position.

2. Select Manual, High Pressure for 40 minutes. When the timer beeps, do a natural pressure release for about 15 minutes.

3. Carefully open the lid and drain the chickpeas with a colander over a large bowl, reserving the cooking liquid.

4. Add the cooked chickpeas, tahini, lemon juice, garlic cloves and salt in a food processor. Process the ingredients until creamy and smooth.

5. Pour about ½ cup of reserved bean liquid, until your desired consistency is achieved. Season with salt and pepper.

6. Serve with your desired toppings and enjoy!

Lentil Soup

Preparation time: 10 minutes

Cook time: 40 minutes

Total time: 50 minutes

Ingredients:

- 1 tsp. of olive oil or vegetable broth
- 1 medium yellow onion, diced
- 3 carrots, chopped
- 3 celery stalks, chopped
- 3 cloves garlic, minced
- 3 Yukon gold potato, diced
- 2 tsp. of herbs of Provence (or fresh herbs)
- 14 ounces of diced tomatoes
- 6 cups of vegetable broth
- 2 cups of green lentils, rinsed
- 3 cups of sliced kale or baby spinach
- 1 tsp. of sea salt
- Black pepper, to taste

Cooking Instructions:

1. Turn the Instant Pot on Sauté function and add the oil or vegetable broth. Cook the onion for 2 minutes, until it starts to brown.

2. Add the carrots, celery, garlic, potato, and herbs and cook for additional 1 minute. Press the Cancel function. Add the tomatoes, broth, and lentils.

3. Close and lock the lid in place and ensure that the valve is in sealing position. Select Manual, High Pressure for 6 minutes.

4. When the timer beeps, do a natural pressure release for about 10 minutes. Carefully open the lid and discard any fresh herb stems.

5. Stir in the kale or spinach until wilted. Season with salt and pepper to taste.

6. Serve immediately and enjoy!

Pulled BBQ Jackfruit

Preparation time: 5 minutes

Cook time: 10 minutes

Total time: 15 minutes

Servings: 6

Ingredients:

- (2) 20 oz. cans of young green jackfruit in brine or water
- 18 oz. of barbecue sauce
- 6 hamburger buns
- Shredded cabbage

Cooking Instructions:

1. Drain and rinse the canned jackfruit, chop off the core portions and discard. Place the jackfruit into the bottom of your Instant Pot and pour 1 cup of water.

2. Close and lock the lid in place and ensure that the valve is in sealing position. Select Manual, High Pressure for 5 minutes.

3. When the timer beeps, do a natural pressure release for about 10 minutes. Carefully open the lid and drain the jackfruit.

4. Place the jackfruit back into the pot. Mash with a potato masher until it resembles pulled meat. Add the barbecue sauce to the pulled jackfruit to make the barbecue sauce.

5. Press the Sauté function. Sauté for about 2 to 5 minutes until warmed through. Serve on buns with shredded cabbage and enjoy!

Black Bean Soup

Preparation time: 10 minutes

Cook time: 40 minutes

Total time: 50 minutes

Serves: 4-6

Ingredients:

- 1 medium red onion, diced
- 3 cloves garlic, minced
- ½ bunch cilantro, stems and leaves divided
- 1 red pepper, diced
- 1 tablespoon of cumin
- 2 tablespoons of chili powder
- ½ teaspoon of cayenne pepper
- 14 ounces dry black beans (about 2 cups)
- 3 cups of vegetable broth, plus extra water
- Juice + zest of 1 lime
- Salt, to taste
- Easy Avocado Salsa, for garnish (Optional)

Cooking Instructions:

1. Add the red onion, garlic, and diced cilantro stems into the bottom of your Instant Pot along with little water.

2. Press the Sauté function and cook the veggies for 2-3 minutes, or until translucent. Add the red pepper and spices and cook for another 2 minutes.

3. Add the dried black beans along with the vegetable broth and give everything a good stir. Gently add enough water to cover the dried Beans.

4. Close and lock the lid in place and ensure that the valve is in sealing position. Select Manual, High Pressure for 30 minutes.

5. When the timer beeps, do a quick pressure release. Carefully open the lid and blend the soup with an Immersion Blender.

6. Serve, topped with your desired topping and enjoy!

Vegetable Bolognese

Servings: 8

Preparation time: 20 minutes

Cook time: 7 minutes

Total time: 42 minutes

Ingredients:

- ½ head of cauliflower, cut into rough florets
- 10 oz. of container mushrooms
- 2 cups of shredded carrot
- 2 cups of eggplant chunks
- 46 oz. of crushed tomatoes
- 1 cup of water
- 6 cloves garlic, minced
- 2 tablespoons of tomato paste
- 2 tablespoons of agave nectar or, your desired sweetener
- 2 tablespoons of balsamic vinegar
- 1 ½ tbsp. of dried oregano
- 1 tablespoon of dried basil
- 1 ½ tsp. of dried rosemary
- Pinch of salt
- Pepper, to taste

Cooking Instructions:

1. In a food processor, add the cauliflower florets and pulse until the pieces are tiny and resembles couscous.

2. Add them into the bottom of your Instant Pot. Add the mushrooms to the food processor and pulse until small. Place them into the Instant Pot.

3. Repeat the same procedure with the carrots and eggplant, until all the veggies are minced and in your Instant Pot liner.

4. Add in the crushed tomatoes, water, garlic, tomato paste, agave nectar, balsamic vinegar, oregano, basil and rosemary.

5. Close and lock the lid in place and ensure that the valve is in sealing position. Select Manual, High Pressure for 7 minutes.

6. When the timer beeps, do a natural pressure release for about 10 minutes. Season with salt and pepper to taste.

7. Add more oregano, basil or rosemary if desired.

8. Serve and enjoy!

Cilantro Lime Quinoa

Preparation time: 5 minutes

Cook time: 10 minutes

Total time: 15 minutes

Servings: 6

Ingredients:

- 1 cup of quinoa, rinsed and drained
- 1 ¼ cups of vegetable broth
- 2 tbsp. of lime juice
- Zest of 1 lime
- ½ cup of chopped cilantro
- Salt to taste

Cooking Instructions:

1. Add the quinoa along with 1 ¼ cup of vegetable broth into the bottom of your Instant Pot. Close and lock the lid in place.

2. Select Manual, High Pressure for 5 minutes. When the timer beeps, do a natural pressure release for about 10 minutes.

3. Carefully open the lid and stir in the lime juice, lime zest, and cilantro. Season with salt, to taste.

4. Serve and enjoy!

Mashed Potatoes with Fried Onions and Bacon

Preparation time: 5 minutes

Cook time: 25 minutes

Total time: 30 minutes

Servings: 8

Ingredients:

- 2 ½ lb. of Yukon potatoes, small
- Enough water to cover
- 2 tbsp. of olive oil
- 4 garlic cloves
- 1 cup of plant milk
- 1 ½ tsp. of salt
- ¼ cup of nutritional yeast
- 1 cup of canned fried onions (We like the ones from Trader Joe's,)
- ½ package or veggie bacon, diced

Cooking Instructions:

1. Wash and rinse the potatoes in clean water. Add the potatoes into the bottom of your Instant Pot and pour about 3 cups of water.

2. Close and lock the lid in place and ensure that the valve is in sealing position. Select Manual, High Pressure for 8 minutes.

3. When the timer beeps, do a natural pressure release for about 10 minutes, then quick release any remaining pressure.

4. Carefully open the lid and drain the potatoes. Press the Sauté function and add the olive oil. Add the bacon, and cook for a couple of minutes.

5. Add the garlic and sauté. Pour 1 cup of milk, salt, and give everything a good stir. Add the potatoes and mash.

6. Add extra milk as desired. Add the fried onions and give everything a good stir to mix.

7. Serve immediately and enjoy!

INSTANT POT APPETIZER RECIPES
Cocktail Wieners

Servings: 4

Preparation time: 10 minutes

Cook time: 1 minute

Total time: 11 minutes

Ingredients:

- 1 pkg. 12 ounces of cocktail wieners
- 1 jar 12 ounces of jalapeno jelly
- ¼ brown sugar
- ¼ cup chili sauce
- ½ cup of chicken or veggie broth
- 1 jalapeno, diced

Cooking Instructions:

1. Add the ½ cup of chicken broth into the bottom of your Instant Pot along with the package of cocktail wieners.

2. Add the brown sugar, jalapeño jelly, diced jalapeños and chili sauce and give everything a good stir to coat.

3. Close and lock the lid in place and ensure that the valve is in sealing position. Select Manual, High Pressure for 1 minute.

4. When the timer beeps, do a quick pressure release. Carefully open the lid and give everything a good stir.

5. Serve and enjoy!

Honey BBQ Wings

Preparation time: 10 minutes

Cook time: 10 minutes

Total time: 20 minutes

Ingredients:

- 1 cup of your desired BBQ sauce
- ½ cup of brown sugar
- 2 tablespoons of Worcestershire sauce
- 1 tablespoon of fresh minced garlic
- ½ cup of water
- ½ cup of honey
- 2 pounds of chicken wings (frozen or thawed)
- ½ tsp. of crushed cayenne pepper, optional

Cooking Instructions:

1. Add all the ingredients into the bottom of your Instant Pot.

2. Close and lock the lid in place and ensure that the valve is in sealing position. Select Manual, High Pressure for 10 minutes.

3. When the timer beeps, do a quick pressure release. Carefully open the lid and place the chicken wings on a pan lined with foil.

4. Baste the chicken wings with more BBQ sauce. Broil them in the oven on high for 5 minutes to caramelize the BBQ.

5. Flip the wings over, baste and then broil for additional 2 minutes.

6. Serve and enjoy!

Cilantro Lime Drumsticks

Preparation time: 5 minutes

Cook time: 15 minutes

Total time: 20 minutes

Servings: 3

Ingredients:

- 1 tablespoon of olive oil
- 6 drumsticks
- 4 cloves minced garlic
- 1 teaspoon of crushed red peppers
- 1 teaspoon of cayenne pepper
- 1 teaspoon of salt ☐ Juice from 1 lime
- 2 tablespoons of chopped cilantro
- ½ cup of chicken broth

Cooking Instructions:

1. Turn the Instant Pot on Sauté function and add the olive oil. Add the drumsticks and sprinkle the seasoning over the drumsticks.

2. Stir the drumsticks to cook and brown on both sides for about 2 minutes. Add the lime juice, cilantro, and chicken broth to the Instant Pot.

3. Close and lock the lid in place and ensure that the valve is in sealing position. Select Manual, High Pressure for 9 minutes.

4. When the timer beeps, do a natural pressure release for about 10 minutes. Carefully open the lid and transfer the drumstick to a baking sheet.

5. Broil the drumsticks until golden brown for about 3-5 minutes. Sprinkle with more cilantro.

6. Serve hot and enjoy!

Bacon Cheeseburger Dip

Preparation time: 10 minutes

Cook time: 4 minutes

Total time: 14 minutes

Ingredients:

- ½ lb. of lean ground beef
- 4-5 slices of bacon, cut into bite sized pieces
- 10 ounces can diced tomatoes with green chili peppers
- 8 ounces of cream cheese, cut into cubes
- 8 ounces of shredded Cheddar-Monterey Jack cheese
- 4 tbsp. of water

Cooking Instructions:

1. Press the Sauté function on your Instant Pot and add the bacon pieces. Sauté the bacon pieces until browned.

2. Transfer the bacon pieces on plate lined with paper towel. Add the ground beef to the pot and sauté until no longer pink.

3. Press the Cancel function and drain off excess grease. Add the bacon, water, diced tomatoes, and cream cheese into the bottom of your Instant Pot and don't stir.

4. Close and lock the lid in place. Select Manual, High Pressure for 4 minutes. When the timer beeps, do a quick pressure release.

5. Carefully remove the lid and stir in cheese. Give everything a good stir to combine. Place in bowl and serve with tortilla chips.

6. Serve and enjoy!

Jalapeno Hot Popper & Chicken Dip

Serves: 10

Preparation time: 3 minutes

Cook time: 12 minutes

Total time: 15 minutes

Ingredients:

- 1 lb. of boneless chicken breast
- 8 ounces cream cheese
- 3 Jalapenos, sliced
- 8 ounces of cheddar cheese
- ¾ cup of sour cream
- ½ cup of panko bread crumbs
- ½ cup of water

Cooking Instructions:

1. Add the chicken breast, sliced Jalapenos, cream cheese and water into the bottom of your Instant pot.

2. Close and lock the lid in place and ensure that the valve is in sealing position. Select Manual, High Pressure for 12 minutes.

3. When the timer beeps, do a quick pressure release. Carefully open the lid and shred the chicken with two forks.

4. Stir in 6 ounces of cheddar cheese and sour cream. Add in a baking dish and top with the rest of the cheese and panko bread crumbs.

5. Place in a broiler and broil for about 2-3 minutes.

6. Serve and enjoy!

Artichoke and Spinach Dip

Serves: 10

Preparation time: 2 minutes

Cook time: 4 minutes

Total time: 6 minutes

Ingredients:

- 8 ounces of cream cheese
- 10 ounces of box Frozen spinach
- 16 ounces of shredded Parm cheese
- 8 ounces of shredded mozzarella
- ½ cup of chicken broth
- 14 ounces can of artichoke hearts
- ½ cup of sour cream
- ½ cup of mayo
- 3 cloves garlic
- 1 teaspoon of onion powder

Cooking Instructions:

1. Add the 3 cloves garlic into the bottom of your Instant Pot along with ½ cup of chicken broth.

2. Drain the artichokes and add them into the Instant Pot. Add the frozen spinach, sour cream, cream cheese, ½ cup of mayo and onion powder in the Instant Pot.

3. Close and lock the lid in place and ensure that the valve is in sealing position. Select Manual, High Pressure for 4 minutes.

4. When the timer beeps, do a quick pressure release. Carefully remove the lid and stir in cheese. Transfer to a serving bowl to thicken as it cools.

5. Serve with corn chips or bread and enjoy!

BBQ Pulled Pork Sliders

Preparation time: 10 minutes

Cook time: 1 hour

Total time: 1 hour 10 minutes

Ingredients:

- ½ cup of soda or apple cider vinegar
- ½ cup of ketchup
- 1/3 cup of brown sugar
- 1 tablespoon of molasses
- 1 tablespoon of Worcestershire sauce
- 3 tablespoons of Cajun or your desired barbecue seasoning
- 5 pounds of pork shoulder
- Coleslaw (I used homemade Dijon Agave Slaw)
- Slider buns, for serving

Cooking Instructions:

1. In a medium bowl, add together the soda or vinegar, ketchup, brown sugar, molasses, and Worcestershire sauce.

2. Add the pork shoulder into the bottom of your Instant Pot and pour the homemade BBQ sauce on top. Sprinkle the seasoning on top of the pork shoulder.

3. Close and lock the lid in place and ensure that the valve is in sealing position. Select Manual, High Pressure for 60 minutes.

4. When the timer beeps, do a natural pressure release for about 10 minutes. Carefully open the lid and shred the pork with two forks.

5. Add more BBQ sauce if you so desire. Serve on slider buns with your desired coleslaw and enjoy!

Chili Con Queso

Preparation time: 10 minutes

Cook time: 5 minutes

Total time: 15 minutes

Ingredients:

- 1.5 pounds of ground chuck
- 1 onion, diced
- 3 - 4 cloves garlic, minced
- 1 (10 ounces) can rotel, undrained
- 1 (15 ounces) can diced tomatoes, undrained
- 1 packet Ortega taco seasoning
- 1 tablespoon of chili powder
- 1 cup of water
- 2 pounds of Velveeta cheese, cut into chunks

Cooking Instructions:

1. Press the Sauté function on your Instant Pot and add the ground beef and onions.

2. Sauté for a couple of minutes until the onion and ground beef is brown. Drain off any excess grease. Add garlic and sauté for additional 1 minute.

3. Add the undrained Rotel, undrained tomatoes, taco seasoning, chili powder, Velveeta chunks and water. Close and lock the lid in place.

4. Select Manual, High Pressure for 5 minutes. When the timer beeps, do a natural pressure release for about 5 minutes.

5. Give everything a good stir to ensure that all Velveeta is melted and combined.

6. Serve warm and enjoy!

Pizza Pull Apart Bread

Preparation time: 10 minutes

Cook time: 10 minutes

Total time: 20 minutes

Ingredients:

- 2 cans of pizza dough, cut into 1-inch strips, then about 1 to 2 inch sections
- 1/3 cup of olive oil
- 2 cups of mozzarella cheese
- 2 tbsp. of fresh parsley chopped
- 4 cloves garlic, minced
- 1 pack mini pepperonis
- Pizza sauce, for dipping

Cooking Instructions:

1. In a medium bowl, combine together the ingredients and toss everything with your hands.

2. Add the ingredients into either spring form pan, or Bundt pan. Pour 1 cup of water into the bottom of your Instant Pot.

3. Place the pan on top of the trivet. Close and lock the lid in place and ensure that the valve is in sealing position.

4. Select Manual, High Pressure for 10 minutes. When the timer beeps, do a quick pressure release. Carefully open the lid and stir.

5. Serve and enjoy!

Sweet and Spicy Meatballs

Preparation time: 5 minutes

Cook time: 25 minutes

Total time: 30 minutes

Ingredients:

- 16 ounces of Cooked Perfect Meatballs
- 12 oz. of chili sauce
- 12 oz. of grape jelly
- ½ cup of water
- ½ tbsp. of crushed red pepper
- ½ tsp. of cayenne pepper
- Chopped green onions, for garnish

Cooking Instructions:

1. Add 16 ounces of Cooked Perfect Meatballs into the bottom of your Instant Pot.

2. In a large bowl, combine together the chili sauce, grape jelly, water and spices and give everything a good stir to combine.

3. Pour the mixture over Cooked Perfect Meatballs and stir to coat. Close and lock the lid in place and ensure that the valve is in sealing position.

4. Select Manual, High Pressure for 10 minutes. When the timer beeps, do a quick pressure release.

5. Carefully remove the lid and allow the meatballs to thicken as it cools. Garnish with chopped green onions, if desired.

6. Serve and enjoy!

INSTANT POT DESSERT RECIPES

Molten Mocha Cake

Preparation time: 10 minutes

Cook time: 25 minutes

Total time: 35 minutes

Serves: 6

Ingredients:

- 1 cup of water
- 4 large eggs
- 1 - ½ cups of sugar
- ½ cup of butter, melted
- 1 tbsp. of vanilla extract
- 1 cup of all-purpose flour
- ½ cup of baking cocoa
- 1 tbsp. of instant coffee granules
- ¼ tsp. of salt
- Fresh raspberries or sliced fresh strawberries and vanilla ice cream, optional

Cooking Instructions:

1. Add water into the bottom of your Instant Pot. In a medium bowl, beat together the eggs, sugar, butter and vanilla until blended.

2. In a separate bowl, whisk together the flour, cocoa, coffee granules and salt; gradually beat into egg mixture. Add the mixture to a greased 1 - 1/2-qt. baking dish.

3. Cover the baking dish with foil and place on a trivet with handles. Place the trivet into the Instant Pot. Close and lock the lid in place and ensure that the valve is in sealing position.

4. Select Manual, High Pressure for 25 minutes. When the timer beeps, do a natural pressure release for about 10 minutes, then quick release any remaining pressure.

5. Carefully open the lid and check for doneness with a toothpick to come out with moist crumbs. If desired, serve warm cake with berries and ice cream.

6. Serve and enjoy!

Cherry & Spice Rice Pudding

Preparation time: 10 minutes

Cook time: 3 minutes

Total time: 13 minutes

Serves: 12

Ingredients:

- 4 cups of cooked rice
- 1 can (12 oz.) evaporated milk
- 1 cup 2% milk
- 1/3 cup of sugar
- ¼ cup of water
- ¾ cup of dried cherries
- 3 tbsp. of butter, softened
- 2 tsp. of vanilla extract
- ½ tsp. of ground cinnamon
- ¼ tsp. of ground nutmeg

Cooking Instructions:

1. Generously grease the Instant Pot inner liner. Add the rice, milks, sugar and water; and give everything a good stir to combine.

2. Add the remaining ingredients. Close and lock the lid in place and ensure that the valve is in sealing position.

3. Select Manual, High Pressure for 3 minutes. When the timer beeps, do a natural pressure release for about 5 minutes, then quick release any remaining pressure.

4. Carefully remove the lid and give everything a good stir.

5. Serve warm or cold. Refrigerate leftovers.

Chocolate Pots de Crème

Preparation time: 10 minutes

Cook time: 6 minutes

Total time: 16 minutes

Ingredients:

- 1 ½ cups of heavy cream
- ½ cup of whole milk
- 5 large egg yolks
- ¼ cup of sugar
- Dash of salt
- 8 oz. of bittersweet chocolate, melted
- Whipped cream and grated chocolate, optional

Cooking Instructions:

1. In a small saucepan, add the cream and milk and bring to a simmer. In a medium bowl, whisk together the egg yolks, sugar, and salt.

2. Gently whisk in the hot cream and milk. Whisk in chocolate until blended. Pour the mixture into 6 custard cups.

3. Pour 1 ½ cups of water into the bottom of your Instant Pot and place the trivet inside. Add the 3 cups on the trivet and place a second trivet on top of the cups.

4. Place the remaining 3 cups on top of the second trivet. Close and lock the lid in place and ensure that the valve is in sealing position.

5. Select Manual, High Pressure for 6 minutes. When the timer beeps, do a natural pressure release for about 15 minutes, then quick release any remaining pressure.

6. Carefully open the lid and transfer the cups to a wire rack to cool. Refrigerate covered with plastic wrap for at least 4 hours or overnight.

7. Serve and enjoy!

Black and Blue Cobbler

Preparation time: 15 minutes

Cook time: 15 minutes

Total time: 30 minutes

Serves: 6

Ingredients:

- 1 cup of all-purpose flour
- 1 - ½ cups of sugar, divided
- 1 tsp. of baking powder
- ¼ tsp. of salt
- ¼ tsp. of ground cinnamon
- ¼ tsp. of ground nutmeg
- 2 large eggs, lightly beaten
- 2 tbsp. of whole milk
- 2 tbsp. of canola oil
- 2 cups of fresh or frozen blackberries
- 2 cups of fresh or frozen blueberries
- ¾ cup of water
- 1 tsp. of grated orange zest
- Whipped cream or vanilla ice cream, optional

Cooking Instructions:

1. Pour 1 cup of water into the bottom of your Instant Pot. In a medium bowl, combine together the flour, ¾ cup of sugar, baking powder, salt, cinnamon and nutmeg.

2. In a separate bowl, combine together the eggs, milk and oil. Pour the mixture into the dry ingredients just until moistened.

3. Generously grease 1-1/2-qt baking dish and spread the batter evenly onto the bottom of the dish. In a large saucepan, combine together the berries, water, orange zest and remaining sugar; bring the pan to a boil.

4. Remove the saucepan from the heat and pour over batter. Loosely cover the baking dish with a piece of aluminum foil. Place the baking dish on top of the trivet.

5. Close and lock the lid in place and ensure that the valve is in sealing position. Select Manual, High Pressure for 15 minutes.

6. When the timer beeps, do a natural pressure release for about 10 minutes, then quick release any remaining pressure.

7. Carefully remove the lid and remove the baking dish. Remove the foil and allow to rest for about 30 minutes before serving.

8. Serve with whipped cream or ice cream if desired.

Arroz Con Leche

Preparation time: 10 minutes

Cook time: 20 minutes

Total time: 30 minutes

Ingredients:

For the Rice:

- 1 cup of white, long grain rice
- 1 ¼ cups of water
- 2 cups of whole milk
- ⅛ teaspoon of salt

Add After Cooking:

- 1 can of sweetened condensed milk
- 1 teaspoon of vanilla extract
- Cinnamon, for topping

Cooking Instructions:

1. Rinse the rice until the water runs clear with a mesh strainer.

2. Add together the milk, water, rice and salt into the bottom of your Instant Pot and give everything a good stir.

3. Close and lock the lid in place and ensure that the valve is in sealing position. Select the Porridge function to cook for 20 minutes.

4. When the timer beeps, do a natural pressure release for about 10 minutes, then quick release any remaining pressure.

5. Carefully remove the lid and add the can of condensed milk and 1 tsp. of vanilla extract. Give everything a good mix.

6. Serve warm and enjoy!

Pumpkin Pie Pudding

Preparation time: 10 minutes

Cook time: 30 minutes

Total time: 40 minutes

Servings: 6

Ingredients:

- 2 eggs
- ½ cup of heavy whipping cream (or almond milk)
- ¾ cup of Erythritol (sub Swerve, Truvia, Splenda or your desired sweetener)
- 15 oz. of canned pumpkin puree
- 1 tsp. of pumpkin pie spice
- 1 tsp. of vanilla
- ½ cup of heavy whipping cream

Cooking Instructions:

1. In a medium bowl, whisk together the 2 eggs and add all remaining ingredients except for heavy whipping cream.

2. Generously grease a 6-inch x 3-inch pan and pour the mixture into the pan. Pour 1.5 cups of water into the bottom of your Instant Pot and place the steamer rack.

3. Add the pan with the pumpkin mixture on top of the steamer rack. Cover the pan with aluminum foil. Close and lock the lid in place.

4. Select Manual, High Pressure for 20 minutes. When the timer beeps, do a natural pressure release for about 10 minutes, then quick release any remaining pressure.

5. Carefully open the lid and remove the pan. Refrigerate for at least 6 hours. Serve with additional whipped cream.

6. Serve and enjoy!

Key Lime Pie

Preparation time: 10 minutes

Cook time: 15 minutes

Total time: 25 minutes

Servings: 8

Ingredients:

For Crust:

- 1 cup graham crackers or vanilla cookies
- 4 tablespoons unsalted butter melted

For Key Lime Filling:

- 3 large egg yolks
- 2/3 cup of key lime juice, about 8-9 key limes
- 1 tbsp. key lime zest, about 2-3 key limes
- 1 (14 ounces) can sweetened condensed milk
- 2 tbsp. of sugar

Topping Ingredients:

- ½ cup of heavy cream
- ¼ cup of sugar
- 1 tsp. of key lime zest, for garnish

Cooking Instructions:

1. Spray a 7" spring form pan with nonstick spray. Place the crackers in a food processor and ground.

2. In a medium bowl, mix together the graham cracker crumbs with the melted butter. Place the mixture into the bottom and sides of the spring form pan.

3. Refrigerate, while making the filling. In a separate bowl, add together the egg yolks and sugar. Pour the egg yolk and sugar mixture in a mixer on medium-high speed.

4. Mix for about 2 minutes or until the yolks turn pale yellow and thicken. Add the condensed milk, key lime juice and zest. Give everything a good mix until combined.

5. Pour this mixture on top of the prepared crust and loosely cover the spring form pan with a piece of aluminum foil.

6. Pour 1 cup of water into the bottom of your Instant Pot and place the trivet inside. Place the spring form pan on top of the trivet.

7. Close and lock the lid in place and ensure that the valve is in sealing position. Select Manual, High Pressure for 15 minutes.

8. When the timer beeps, do a natural pressure release for about 10 minutes. Carefully open the lid and remove the spring form pan.

9. Remove the aluminum foil cover and the center should be a bit jiggly. Refrigerate for at least 4 hours.

10. Top with the whip cream and slowly add the sugar until the cream becomes stiff, if desired. Pipe on top of pie and decorate with zest.

11. Serve and enjoy!